D1259655

AN ARTIST ON MIGRATION

Bruce Pearson

HarperCollins*Publishers*

HarperCollins*Publishers*
London · Glasgow · Sydney
Auckland · Toronto · Johannesburg

TO THE MEMORY
OF CRISPIN FISHER

First published 1991

10 9 8 7 6 5 4 3 2 1
94 93 92 91

ISBN 0 00 219814 2

Colour reproduction by
J Film Processing, Bangkok, Thailand
Printed and Bound in Italy by
Printed in Italy by G. Canale & C. S.p.A. - Borgaro T.se - Torino

Contents

Acknowledgements

I owe a debt of gratitude to many people who have helped me in the course of preparing this book. In particular I would like to thank Dave Orchard for his companionship and the enormous efforts he made to get us both safely through Africa. The book pivoted around his contribution and our African adventure. I would also like to thank Jamie Skinner for his help in Africa, and for checking the text on his return; Angus Erskine of Erskine Expeditions who generously gave me access to Greenland; Robert Burton who I accompanied to Greenland and who also shared some great moments and some of the driving during other field-trips; Jack and Jane Sheldon, David Norman and others of the Morecambe Bay Ringing Group for their help and hospitality, and Phil Ireland and the Wash Wader Ringing Group for theirs; Dr Robin Baker for allowing me to quote from his book and for commenting on some draft text; Walter Hartmut for allowing me to quote a passage from his book on Eleonora's Falcon. Fieldwork was helped along, or guidance and information freely given by Nico Dekker, Kees Boot, Oene Moedt, Denis Bredin, Mick Rogers, Pete Gotham, Bob Image, Roger Clarke, Tony Salmon, Peter Prince, Redland Aggregates Ltd, Holger Schultz, Humphrey Crick, Peter Reid, Mike Moser and Jean-Yves Pirot of the International Waterfowl and Wetlands Research Bureau (IWRB) and Dr. Stephen Baillie of the British Trust for Ornithology (BTO). I would also like especially to thank Chris Mead, Ringing and Migration Officer at the BTO who fired a rapid succession of suggestions at me when I first mentioned the idea and who was kind enough to read through the text when I had finished. I would also like to thank Wim Verheught and Tobias Salathé of the International Council for Bird Preservation (ICBP). At the Royal Society for the Protection of Birds (RSPB) I would like to thank Alistair Gammell and the International Department, Mike Everett, Chris Harbard, Richard Porter and the Librarian Ian Dawson. Thanks also to Mike Shaw at Curtis Brown for his help in making the idea a reality, and to Brian Jackman for his comments and suggestion on the final draft. Finally, I would have liked Crispin Fisher at Collins to have seen the finished book. As the publisher, his enormous enthusiasm for the idea when I first showed it to him, at its egg stage, made the long incubation period possible; his untimely death occurred as the book was hatching. The fact that it has at last taken wing is due to the equal enthusiasm and support of Myles Archibald at Collins.

CHAPTER ONE

Awakening

Returning to old haunts with adult eyes is a dangerous thing to do. Things remembered tend to look small and unimpressive leaving you disappointed and wondering why you ever bothered to go back in the first place. But today I have returned to the meres at Framlingham in Suffolk – and for good reason. It is not to wander nostalgically down the tracks and trails of boyhood, but today is March 21st, officially the first day of spring, and I am looking specifically for birds and a sense of changing seasons in an ancient and watery landscape.

As a schoolboy twenty five years ago I escaped to these meres whenever I could. Between mornings of maths or French, or afternoons of rugby or detention, I rushed away to splash around and map nesting sites of coots and blackbirds, robins and moorhens. Here I caught my first ever glimpse of a kingfisher, and in my last summer term I watched a pair of whitethroats raise a brood. I remember the willow trees – enormous heavy-limbed trees, sometimes sagging down into the water, then sweeping up with slender branches to light and lofty crowns. The tallest trees were in the overgrown corner below the church. There were alders and hawthorn thickets as well, that spread with the willows in a ragged circle round the outside edge of the meres. Filling the ring of trees was a patchwork of grasses and sedge. In the middle was open water. Whichever way you walked around the meres the ruin of Framlingham castle, rising high on its ancient mound on the eastern side, dominated the landscape.

With a small, dog-eared sketch-pad, and a growing interest in drawing and natural history, it was a great place to spend my free time – an ancient wetland right on my doorstep and filled with a sense of mystery, excitement, and plenty of birds. Here I learned about the comings and goings of our winter and summer birds. I cannot remember specifically, but I would like to think that I wondered where Swallows went to each winter. I can certainly remember spending hours trying to learn more about birds by leafing through the three volumes of T. A. Coward's *Birds of the British Isles and their Eggs*, pausing to copy some of Thorburn's superb colour plates.

The views today across the meres are as impressive as anything I remember, and I am far from disappointed by returning. The morning was dark and showery with a cold wind that turned one shower to hail, but by now, in late afternoon, the cloud has lifted and the rain has held off long enough for me to get on with some work. As I have sat painting I have been watching the seasonal mix of winter and spring in the wildlife and landscape.

March 21st at Framlingham Meres, Suffolk. Waiting for sight or sound of the first spring migrants.

Although some early individuals will have passed through already, any day now the first trickle of summer migrants will be arriving. Wisps of snipe have risen frequently to chase around the meres, and then have dropped back in to the thick vegetation at the water margins to resume their rasping calls. Out on the open water are tufted duck and mallard in pairs, and strung along a fallen log is a neat row of black-headed gulls, most of them still in winter plumage, but there are two that are wearing their summer hood of chocolate brown. There are celandines and primroses flowering on the sheltered banks of the castle mound and there is a hint of new leaf in some of the hawthorns. In the middle of one of mears two agitated coots have been busy disputing a territorial boundary, rushing at each other with heads lowered and wings arched. A pair of blackbirds copulating on a willow bough is final confirmation that it is spring, but reminders of winter linger in the landscape. Chattering their way down a thick stand of hawthorn on the far side is a small flock of fieldfares, winter visitors that will shortly be making their way home to Scandinavia.

Soon, floods of watery evening light are squeezing through gaps in the cloud, and the wind drops. A party of long-tailed tits bounces through the willow tops and I can hear a wren working its way through a bramble and hawthorn thicket behind me, its progress given away every now and then by its sharp rattling musical call. Then from the thick scrub, further down the meres towards the town, comes one of the most distinctive sounds of the early year, and one that I have been waiting for since last autumn – *chiff ...chiff*.. ...*chiff*...*chaff*...*chaff*...*chiff* – a chiffchaff is calling. With an increasing number of these small unobtrusive warblers overwintering in southern Britain and Europe each year, I cannot be sure that this one has just made a journey from southern Europe or Africa – but no matter. For as Viscount Grey of Fallodon wrote over 50 years ago, the first chiffchaff of the spring is 'a symbol, a promise, an assurance of what is to come.'

It seems to me that the meres have changed little in twenty-five years and it is easy to imagine that the landscape will have remained virtually unaltered since the very earliest settlement was founded here almost 2000 years ago. Every spring for a thousand years or more, swallows will have arrived to spend the summer hawking for insects over the water. House martins will have come to build their nests under the overhangs in the castle walls. Willow and sedge warblers, whitethroats and turtle doves will have made their summer homes in the surrounding nettles, willows, hawthorn and oaks that surround these meres. For thousands of years, when the summer visitors departed, winter visitors like redwings and fieldfares will have arrived to strip the berries from the hawthorns. People who settled here down the centuries would have hunted the wild birds of the meres and understood that they changed with the seasons. Perhaps they would have seen their movements as part of the annual cycle on which their lives depended. What they could not have known however, was the enormous distances some of the birds had travelled and the complex patterns of migration that had brought them here. Human awareness of the migratory phenomenon goes back thousands of years, an understanding of the truth behind the seasonal disappearance of birds has come about only in the past 200 years or so.

The earliest written evidence which suggests that bird migration had caught the human imagination, comes from the eastern end of the Mediterranean and Middle East. Today this area sees one of the most spectacular concentrations of migrant birds in the world, as the region funnels hundreds of thousands of birds travelling from Europe and Asia towards Africa. In Homer's Iliad written in about 1000 BC. the Trojan army in retreat is compared to the fleeing of Cranes ahead of the approaching winter:

> *Like unto birds, even as when there goeth up before heaven a clamour of cranes which flee from the coming of winter and sudden rain.*

The Prophet Jeremiah knew that migrants like storks and swallows had their 'appointed times'. Although migration patterns and numbers will have changed over the millenia, there is little doubt that similar scenes of large and conspicuous flocks of soaring birds would have been observed by people of the ancient world.

There are Biblical passages that refer to the seasonal flight of birds. Turtle doves are included in a celebration of winter's passing, and the Book of Job refers to raptor migration.

In Roman times there appears to have been knowledge of the navigational skills of birds. Attending the chariot races in Rome, a nobleman took Swallows with him from his home in Valena. After each race, a bird was released carrying a small token of the winning colours tied to its leg so news of the result could be quickly conveyed back to his villa.

The first systematic approach to understanding bird migration was made by Aristotle 2300 years ago, who drew together the many threads of legend that trailed away into antiquity. He borrowed from other classical writers and also included many of his own quite accurate observations, such as how the Cuckoo departed early in July soon after breeding, and referred to the fact that "..all creatures are fatter in migrating". He appreciated too, that; as men of great possessions spend their summer in cool places and their winter in sunny ones, so also all animals that can do so shift their habitat at various seasons. Some creatures can make provision against change without stirring from their ordinary haunts.

In the light of present knowledge many of Aristotle's ideas and observations were quite sound, but then he managed to add a few highly fanciful embellishments. He was also sure that:

> *A great number of birds also go into hiding; they do not all migrate, as is generally supposed, to warmer countries.*

He believed hibernation and transmutation could explain the departure and arrival of some species.

Although the idea of bird hibernation might seem highly fanciful, it is quite easy to see how it could have developed in the ancient world from a mis-interpreted behavioural observation of a mis-identified species.

Swifts, for example, nest in holes and for a time the young are naked. During periods of cold wet weather the parent birds may be forced to forage far from the nest for long periods. To cope with several days of starvation in the nest, young swifts become torpid and their temperature drops from the normal 101°F to as low as 70°F. A mis-identified swift becoming a hibernating swallow is therefore perhaps understandable.

The theory of transmutation to account for the disappearance of birds could be explained equally logically by a scholarly mind working behind an eye untrained in the subtleties of immature plumages and moult patterns of birds. For example, redstarts are common summer visitors to Greece and the robin is an abundant winter visitor. They are closely related and in some plumages are similarly sized and coloured. As autumn approaches the number of redstarts

The Bosphorus in Turkey is a channel less than 2 kilometres wide and almost 30 kilometres long that links the Black Sea to the Sea of Marmara. This narrow waterway lies at the confluence of migratory streams of enormous numbers of eagles, buzzards and storks making their way each autumn from Europe towards Asia and Africa. Between the end of July and early October over 70,000 white and 60,000 black storks, 10,000 buzzards, 2,000 honey buzzards and 1000 short-toed eagles and numerous other birds cross this ancient divide.

The migratory stream of large soaring birds is not continuous throughout the season, or from day to day, or during the daylight hours. Different species have different seasons for their passage; late August and early September at the Bosphorus sees the largest numbers of honey buzzards and storks. By mid-September Levant sparrowhawks are numerous, then in late September come the eagles and buzzards and small parties of Egyptian and griffon vultures. Being dependent on thermals they can only travel at times of the day when thermalling conditions are most favourable – so nothing much moves in early morning or from late afternoon onwards. On wet and stormy days when movement is slowed to a trickle or halted completely, a great torrent of birds sets off as soon as conditions improve. In north-east Turkey 137,000 birds of prey were recorded passing in one day as they continued their migration after being halted by a period of heavy rain.

dwindles as they migrate south; at the same time the number of Robins reaching Greece to winter begins to increases. Behold – the transmutation of birds!

The formidable authority of Aristotle's writings ensured that transmutation and hibernation dominated the thinking and interpretation of migration for almost 2000 years.

During the Dark Ages and Mediaeval period in Europe, the necessity of hunting wild birds and the development of falconry as a sport would have led to a deeper understanding of their ways. Emperor Frederick II of Hohenstaufen (1194–1250) wrote a treatise on falconry that revealed a great knowledge of natural history, and although his work deals chiefly with birds of prey and quarry species, it also included information on bird migration.

A little over 200 years later Johann Wonnecke von Caub in Germany noted that the stork heralds the spring and loves to be with human beings. He added that storks travelled across the sea in large numbers into Asia and warm regions. But at the same time he was equally convinced that Swallows seek mountain peaks when they leave for the winter and can be found there, "all bare and without feathers". Transmutation as an explanation for migration withered early in the ornithological debate. In 15th century Europe it seemed that the hibernation theory ruled the day with more and more bizarre 'facts' being put forward in support of it. The most frequently quoted of the 'lunatic fringe' of hibernationists is Olaus Magnus, who was Bishop of Uppsala in Sweden. In 1555 he published a slim volume which contained some remarkable observations concerning the seasonal whereabouts of swallows.

> *Several authors who have written at length about the inestimable facts of nature, have described how Swallows often fly from one country to another, travelling to a warm climate for the winter months; but they have not mentioned the denizens of northern regions which are often pulled from the water by fishermen in a large ball. They cling beak to beak, wing to wing, foot to foot, having bound themselves together in the first days of autumn in order to hide amid canes and reeds. It has been observed that when spring comes they return joyously to their old nests or build new ones, according to the dictates of nature. Occasionally young fishermen, unfamiliar with these birds, will bring up a large ball and carry it to a stove, where heat dissolves it into swallows.*

Perhaps his conclusions about swallows were based on original observations. Swallows sometimes gather at dusk to roost in reedbeds, crowding together in astonishing numbers, even bending stems down into the water.

From the confusion of ideas and fanciful conclusions advanced in these early years, a small but growing number of ornithologists were beginning to come to some quite original conclusions.

In England one of the first and most celebrated of the early 'migrationists' was William Turner, named by some as the father of British ornithology. Ten years before Olaus Magnus's famous publication, Turner produced a

March 10th. Swallows arriving 'home' over Ballard Down in Dorset.

work which, although it drew much from the theories of Pliny and Aristotle, was a critical revision of their traditional authority. Much of it he rejected. Turner was also an excellent field ornithologist able to recognise difficult to distinguish birds (for his times) such as hen and marsh harrier, or meadow pipit and woodlark. He recorded the autumn arrival of redwings, and noted the fieldfares feeding on the berries during the winter.

Pierre Belon, a Frenchman, travelled widely through the eastern Mediterranean and Asia Minor in the 16th century and was able to observe migrants on the move and in their winter quarters. Referring to white storks, he wrote

> *It is definite they spend the winter in Egypt and Africa, for we have seen the Egyptian plains white with them in September and October, so numerous they were.*

About swallows he accurately concluded;

> *As swallows cannot spend the winter in Europe because of the great cold and because they would not find food, they go to Africa, Egypt and Arabia, where, since winter resembles our summer, they have no lack of nourishment.*

A little over a 100 years after the publication of Olaus Magnus's book, a bright light began to shine on the growing ornithological debate. Its source was The Reverend John Ray (1627–1705) who is considered to have been both the 'father of modern zoology' and 'perhaps the greatest of all field naturalists'. He travelled widely throughout the British Isles and Europe, mostly in company with his great friend Francis Willoughby. With Willoughby's support, and under Ray's main authorship, Francis Willoughby's *Ornithologica* was published in Latin in 1676, with the English version *The Ornithology of F.W. Willoughby* appearing in 1678. The work was a critical review of existing knowledge, that with the addition of their field notes and collections, brought a new sophistication to the status, identification and distribution of birds. They described the migration of ruffs, the passage of raptors over the Bosphorus, and the autumn arrival in Britain of fieldfares and redwings from Scandinavia. They were sure that hibernation had no part to play in the seasonal appearance and disappearance of birds and, taking up the recurring idea of hibernating swallows, they wrote

> *What becomes of Swallows in the Winter time, wether they fly into other Countries, or lie torpid in hollow trees, and the like places, neither are Natural Historians agreed, nor can we certainly determine. To us it seems more probable that they fly away into hot Countries, viz. Egypt, Æthiopia etc. than that they either lurk in hollow trees, or holes of rocks and ancient buildings, or lie in water under the ice in Northern Countries, as Olaus Magnus reports.*

With the significant contribution of Ray and Willoughby, the 17th century can be considered to be the first century of the science of ornithology, even though the debate between those who believed in hibernation and those who supported the idea of migration still continued. Even in the 18th century swallows were still being imprisoned in greenhouses. After some considerable time it was apparent that they had no interest in hibernating so they were released. Other swallows kept in conditions ideal for torpidity soon died.

Although he was sometimes doubtful, Gilbert White believed largely in bird migration, being "always seized with wonder, and long to be informed, whence these travellers come and wither they go, since they seem to use our hills merely as an inn or resting place". The debate reached a bizarre level in correspondence published in the *Gentleman's Magazine* in 1759. "Many are the times that Swallows have been watched retiring to hibernation," wrote the naturalist M. Kline. "They take hold of one another's feet, roll themselves up, throw themselves into the water and presently sink. Why, one observer of good reputation has recorded that Swallows will sing for as long as an hour before catching hold of one another and diving into the water".

But perhaps after all it was Aristotle who was to have the last laugh. A little more than 100 years after the controversy had been settled in favour of the migration theory, echoes of the 2000 year old debate suddenly reverberated from a rock crevice in the Colorado Desert in America. In the winter of 1946, and in the two winters that followed, an American nightjar called a Nuttall's poorwill was found squeezed into a rock crevice in the heart of

CUCKOO

To an untutored eye, the sharp-winged and long-tailed silhouette of the cuckoo is frequently confused with a kestrel or sparrowhawk; to an untuned ear its call can be confused with a cooing collared dove. Consequently, the 'first cuckoo of spring' is often announced before its arrival and false reports are so frequent that March cuckoos are looked upon with suspicion.

For centuries this melodic herald of summer has had an ambiguous place in European fable, folklore and legend. Its parasitic breeding habits ensured that it was seen both as an adulterer, and a synonym for ingratitude. But it also shares with the swallow the honour of being the welcome ambassador of spring.

In the British Isles there was a traditional belief that if the cuckoo was captured as it arrived with the spring, then the better weather it brought with it could be caught and held to relieve the gloom of winter later on. There are still isolated spots known as 'cuckoo pens'.

The northward migration of the cuckoo across Europe is reflected in the traditional days when it is expected in different countries. In southern France it is March 21st and in northern France April 1st. In Germany the traditional day is 14th April, and further north in Norway the day is May 1st. In southern England, where the traditional day is 14th April, Gilbert White's earliest date was 7th April, and his latest was 26th April.

the desert. Its body temperature was very low and it was in a torpid condition – in fact, the bird was hibernating!

From the middle of the 19th century onwards, the migration of birds was generally recognised and the scientific debate moved quickly to discussing Why do birds migrate? What species are involved? How do they find their way?

Since the time when Gilbert White had watched and carefully noted the seasonal changes of birds in Wiltshire 200 years ago, it was evident to a number of ornithologists in Britain that the direct observation of birds in the field was important to the study of migration.

In the 1870s John Alexander Harvie-Brown used a cooperative investigation technique that centralised the gathering of migration information by circulating questionnaires to lighthouse keepers and other isolated observers who were asked to log their observations. When the results were looked at together, the broad patterns of migration became more apparent.

Coordinated observations at fixed points at definite times of day when the weather conditions are known, provides a wealth of information about the identity of species, their numbers and direction of flight; but it was realised that individual birds must be caught and uniquely marked to better understand bird migration. By capturing or recovering the bird at some future date as it made its journey or arrived at its destination, it would be possible to obtain very precise information. The more birds marked and the more re-captured, the more accurate would be the overall picture.

In America during the 18th century James Audubon had begun 'ringing' birds with a light silver thread with some success. A swallow shot in Yorkshire in the 19th century was found to have a tiny piece of parchment attached to its leg bearing the words: J. Pornina y Clavi, Barcelona, 10th March, 1845. But it was not until the very end of the 19th century that attempts at serious scientific bird marking were made and the first of these were made in Europe.

In 1891 Christian Mortensen, a Danish ornithologist, began fixing thin pieces of zinc to the legs of birds but found that the birds seemed to find these uncomfortable. Later on, however, he had greater success by using light-weight aluminium rings, each one bearing the date and locality of the experiment. He was given considerable encouragement when a ring from a merganser, which had been shot some distance away, was returned to him. This resulted in him developing a more ambitious ringing programme that was operational by 1899.

By coincidence, in the year that Mortensen began his experiments with zinc rings in Denmark, a man called Heinrich Gätke published a book in his native Germany entitled *Die Vogelwarte Helgoland* which appeared in English in 1895 as *Heligoland as an Ornithological Observatory*. Gätke was not a trained scientist but a great field naturalist, and for much of his life he lived on the tiny island of Helgoland, which lies 60km north of the German mainland in the south-eastern corner of the North Sea. For fifty years, 'day after day, the seasons through, he walked his small kingdom, observing acutely'. He was keenly aware that weather influenced the migration of birds, and at a time when the existence of narrow migration routes was widely believed, he proposed that huge numbers of birds migrated on a broad front, something that was later shown to be the case.

The significant parallel developments of Mortensen's ringing work and Gätke's bird observatory were soon taken up by others and it was not long before the two concepts were brought together. In 1901 the German Ornithological Society established a bird observatory at Rossitten, an island at the eastern end of the Baltic, and within two years they had introduced the recently perfected technique of bird ringing.

In Britain, migration research in the decades that spanned the turn of the century had taken a different route. Although H.F. Witherby, who at that time was the proprietor of the monthly journal *British Birds*, and Professor Landsborough Thomson of Aberdeen University, had both introduced ringing schemes in 1909, ornithologists were still mainly concerned with survey work and cooperative investigation techniques.

Harvie-Browne's pioneering work showed clearly that headlands and islands are particularly well placed to study migration, and the British Association for the Advancement of Science followed on by sponsoring a survey that collected and analysed bird reports from lighthouse keepers. In 1901 William Eagle Clarke began a survey of remote and wild islands at migration time. More ambitious programmes followed, collecting and analysing observations from lighthouse keepers and linked to information from observers stationed inland.

However, it was not until 1933 that Britain's first bird observatory was established 'almost by accident'. Six years earlier R. M. Lockley had gone to Skokholm, a small uninhabited island off the western tip of Wales, to live the life of a shepherd and fisherman, as well as to study the abundant seabirds on the island. After publishing some early results of his work, the importance of its location and bird life was soon realised by others and Skokholm was soon invaded by a number of keen and like-minded ornithologists. The director of the Vogelwarte Helgoland in Germany sent plans of a large trap that they had in use there for catching birds, and by the autumn of 1933 Britain's first Heligoland trap was operating successfully on Skokholm. Within a year a second trap had been built, this time by the Midlothian Ornithological Club on the Isle of May, a small island lying in the Firth of Forth on the east coast of Scotland.

The pace of research was quickening. By 1937 it was clear that in the British Isles an independent ringing scheme would be more effective. That year Harry Witherby, who had cancelled the Aberdeen University scheme some years earlier, transferred control to the Bird Ringing Committee of the newly formed British Trust for Ornithology – the BTO. With a fledgling observatory network, and a single ringing scheme in the British Isles, the stage was set for increasingly rapid advances in understanding of the migratory phenomenon.

In February 1946 a pioneering group of observatory and ringing enthusiasts attended the first meeting of the Bird Observatories Committee. It was at this meeting that the definition of a bird observatory was given as 'A field station co-operatively manned for the purpose of making continuous observations on migrant birds, and for catching, examining and marking them.' Of necessity it is a clear, precise and perhaps academic definition that to me somehow fails to hint at the drama and excitement that is an observatory operating at peak migration time.

Not being a ringer myself, I have nevertheless watched excitedly at a number of observatories, experiencing first-hand fragments of the vast migration story falling into place. Each tiny bright-eyed warbler in the hand set me thinking about how long was its journey and how had it found the energy. What problems had it faced with the weather? But it was also time spent birding and painting in Africa over a number of years that set me thinking about bird migration.

Swallows over a reed-bed at dusk.

Among the host of colourful local species I sometimes caught sight of species familiar to me from 'home', and other times more unusual birds from much further east in Europe and Asia.

On one hand the naturalist in me began to ponder the routes that they might have followed as they travelled between their seasonal homes in temperate and tropical regions. I wondered how they found their way, did they fly by night and steer by the stars, or travel by day and use the sun as a compass? How many birds were involved each year and how many survived the journey? Were those migrants familiar to me from 'home' either African species that visited us each summer, or were they Palearctic species that took refuge in Africa each winter? Which was their ancestral 'home'?

The artist in me on the other hand visualised the changing landscapes and seasons the birds experienced as they made their journeys. I wondered what parts of Africa different species visited, and why? I was interested in knowing what habitats in Africa actually looked like. What were the colours of mid-winter in the Sahel? What did the Guinea and the Sudan savannas look like after the rains had passed?

Back in my old familiar birding haunts in Britain similar questions and comparisons increasingly came to mind as I watched and contemplated different species. Where had that dunlin flock wintered, and where would their summer home be? I questioned the seasonal homes of the grey plovers, whimbrel, sanderling and bar-tailed godwits I sketched on the coast during the migration seasons. Some would have been heading to or coming from the high arctic tundra of Greenland or the forest bog mosaic of northern Scandinavia. What were those landscapes like?

By now almost obsessed by the idea of bird migration, I delved deeper into the wealth of migration literature searching for at least some of the answers. Soon I realized that the subject was so vast and complex that it would take a lifetime to really understand it because I am no academic but an artist. Nevertheless, although images of the contrasting life and landscapes of birds on migration constantly kept coming to mind, I found the ornithological story, or the science of migration that explained what I was seeing, equally fascinating.

To try and tell that story and convey some of the excitement I felt, I wondered if it was possible to journey with the migrants with my studio on my back. Firstly northwards to the high arctic tundra, then south through Europe into the heart of Africa? Rather than simply an illustrated diary, there could be explanations that linked the underlying scientific story to the narrative and to the paintings of the birds and landscapes I encountered along the way. An artist on migration could not be the complete story of bird migration, only my story or interpretation of parts of it. To begin the story I had sat for a day at Framlingham meres trying to see migration as people long ago might have done. If ever in spring, a stretch of water should spawn soggy clusters of awakening swallows, then that ancient and mysterious waterlogged hollow in Suffolk is where it will happen. At the Bosphorus I had watched the spectacle of migration, a sight that similarly must have inspired the ancients. Now, with spring already here, and the first few migrants already arriving, I must be on my way.

CHAPTER TWO

Home At Last and Passing Through

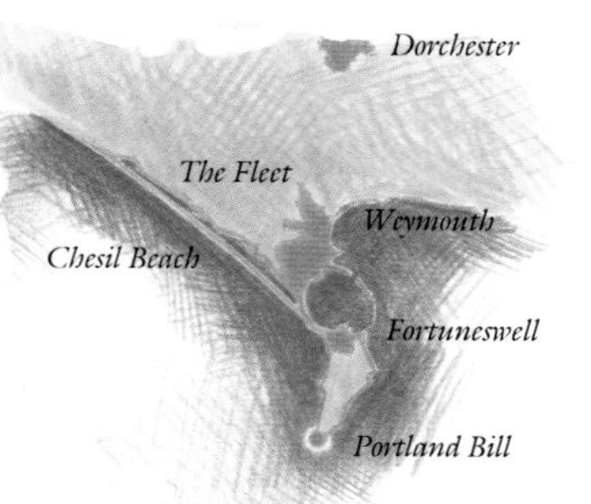

Yesterday I drove down to Dorset through thin flurries of snow – the last cold sting in winter's tail. It was the 8th of April. I slept overnight in the van, which is a kind of mobile studio and home, fully equipped for following birds on migration. It has plenty of space for paints and easel, a bunk bed, stoves and lockers full of food.

Before first light I made my way from the campsite above the Fleet, down through the empty streets of Weymouth and drove south on the road which runs along the Chesil Bank towards Portland. At the end the road climbs steeply up onto the island, and in the darkness I followed it over the top and out towards the Bill.

Portland is a massive limestone slab that slopes down and tapers from a broad north face of steep cliffs to a stubby bouldered finger at Portland Bill. The Bill points across the English Channel towards the nearest landfall, the Channel Islands and the Cherbourg peninsula of France, over 100 kilometres to the south. Hanging some distance offshore from its thick shingle thread, Portland is an ideal place to watch the migration of birds.

On the seaward side of the path that winds around the end of the Bill lies a mass of boulder debris strewn around inlets and wave-cut platforms. On the landward side are gently sloping grassy commons where the soil is thin and rocks break through. The commons are strewn with bramble thickets – tight thorny domes that are as sharp as rusty bundles of barbed-wire. Higher up the slope is a row of cottages, a public house and a prickly cluster of military buildings, its humming mast and aerials wrapped tight in a high security fence. Portland Bill is not a romantic landscape; it has a functional, hard worn and an obvious military air.

As I walked down the path near the end of the Bill, first light reveals a clear sky with only a few high wisps of cloud. Last night will have been a good one for birds to be travelling.

The earlier snow flurries have left no trace on the ground. The wind, which is still blustery and bitterly cold from the northeast, whines through the wires and rumbles around the enormous bulk of the lighthouse. It carries too the tidal roar of the Portland Race tearing around the end of the Bill.

Wheatears are the first to appear in the growing light, flitting and bobbing along the boulders and rocks around the shoreline, with some moving around on the short grass of the low cliff tops. High overhead I can see other birds in ones and twos heading inland, then small flocks just visible out over the sea. Some of these long distance travellers are too far off to safely identify and any audible clues are being swept away in the sound of sea and wind. Then passing close by, unnoticed until it is within earshot, is a tree pipit bounding inland with its long loping flight.

Suddenly a ring ouzel appears among the boulders just below me – I failed to see it over the sea, or notice where it landed on the shore, but moments later there is another; both are males. They will have wintered in southern Spain or north-west Africa and, travelling this far west, they are almost certainly birds heading for a breeding site in open moorland or fell country in Britain; continental birds would be much further east.

As the light fills and the sun warms, a skylark climbs high into the wind and hangs there singing. A jackdaw carrying a bundle of dried grass passes overhead towards the nest it must be building on the sheer western cliffs. From telephone wires and bramble tops greenfinches make short excursions to sing and display. For the birds like these that did not venture to distant lands last winter, the breeding season is already underway – for most of the migrants there is still a long journey ahead.

Early morning arrival of a wheatear at Portland Bill.

The Heligoland trap and Portland Bird Observatory.

In the first hour of daylight there is a noticeable increase in the number of arriving birds visible all over the Bill. Handfuls of swallows have appeared in the wind, and the bramble and blackthorn thickets are busy with redstarts, blackcaps and willow warblers. But it is the change in the wheatears that is particularly noticeable. Now there are many more, but I can find none along the edge of the sea and cliffs. Instead, they have moved on to the short grass of the commons where I can see about fifteen or twenty wheatears feeding. Interestingly, all but two are males.

In many species of small migrant that travel north in spring the male birds move northwards before the females. This is advantageous to the male as they reach the breeding grounds earlier, acquire a better territory and thus increase their chance of attracting a mate.

Close to the southern tip of Portland rises the massive red and white banded lighthouse tower that guides modern shipping. In earlier times it was a combination of Higher and Lower Lighthouses that warned mariners. The Old Lower Lighthouse, which still stands well back from the sea on the eastern side of the Bill, has for 30 years been the home of the Portland Bird Observatory. The observatory, like many others in the network throughout the country, offers accommodation and laboratory facilities to many professional and amateur enthusiasts of migration. As well as those functional and scientific facilities, observatories also offer a great social experience and for anyone with more than a passing interest in birds, are just great places to be – they represent birding 'at the sharp end' where much of the action is.

At the Observatory this morning they will have been catching and ringing birds since just before dawn – it is time to find out what has been happening. The walled garden of the observatory is long and narrow and slopes down towards the sea. At the top end of the garden stands the ringing hut, and almost filling the middle is a Heligoland trap encased in a dense tangle of brambles, elder and sea buckthorn. Bright early morning sunlight streams in through the open door of the ringing hut lighting up a hive of activity inside. I unfold my sketching stool and sit down in a corner to watch.

At the desk on the far side the observatory warden Mick Rogers takes a bag from a peg on the wall beside him and gently extracts a bird. "Chiffchaff" he says to the fellow sitting behind him who is logging the details of each bird, then adds, "with pollen". Pulling a small metal ring in the shape of an open 'C' from a string of others, he reads aloud the ring number and then places it around the bird's leg. He butts the two open ends of the ring together, and then with a pair of special pliers carefully squeezes the ends tight, leaving the ring loose but secure on the chiffchaff's leg.

Catching and ringing birds is a very skilled operation conducted mostly by enthusiastic and dedicated amateurs. The training to the high standards required for a license is a strictly controlled and lengthy business; the reason is obvious. It is totally pointless marking birds that have been damaged in nets or by badly applied rings – the whole purpose of the exercise is to investigate healthy wild bird populations. The light-metal ring that the bird wears bears a unique serial number and a postal address so that when it is re-trapped or the ring found, the number can be fed back into the mass of ringing data held by the British Trust for Ornithology (BTO), the organisation responsible for all ringing in Britain. Many other countries have ringing schemes, and although each stores its own ringing information, there is a continuous flow of data between them. To date, well over 120 million birds have been ringed worldwide, and the number increases by 4 or 5 million each year.

Still holding the chiffchaff, Mick measures the wing length, then slipping the bird quickly into a plastic cone attached to a spring balance, he reads the bird's weight. "Wing 59 millimetres and weight 7.1 grams" he says, opening a small trap door in the front wall of the hut and releasing the chiffchaff back into the warm spring sunshine.

From capture to release the whole process for that one bird has taken perhaps five or six minutes – a slight inconvenience to one individual warbler, but if it is found again the exact geographical location of the bird will be known twice in its life. But, while the bird is captive, it will have been weighed, sexed and measured, and its state of moult will have been noted, so maximising the information obtained from each individual bird. If enough birds are caught and 'processed' for information they will help build a picture of not only the species' migratory habits, but also many other detailed aspects of their lives.

However, only a minute percentage of the many millions of birds bearing rings will ever be recovered. The chances are greater with bigger birds and in more densely populated temperate lands, but in sparsely populated and remote areas of the tropics, the probability of a ringed bird being recovered is virtually nil – but still there is always a chance. A hunter in the Cameroons who shot a cuckoo bearing a ring handed it in a few days later to a mission station 300 kilometres from his village; but that was in the 1930s and remains the only record so far from that remote part of Africa.

As well as the Heligoland trap, mist nets are in use at the observatory this morning, and as the nets suddenly begin to fill, it is apparent that a ripple of migrants is passing through after the larger waves of earlier this morning. In the space of half-an-hour 40 birds are caught and the nets must be checked frequently.

One of the assistants hurries into the hut holding a cluster of bird bags and hangs each one on a peg along the end wall. There is a female blackbird, a few dunnocks, a goldcrest and a greenfinch or two, but most of them are willow warblers, including the first definite female of the year. Until now all had been males and, like the male wheatears, racing ahead to secure territories.

The last bird in this catch is another warbler – the processing continues again – "Male blackcap.... a five.... with pollen," says Mick. The number five is the bird's age code (the numbers running from one to nine) and means that this blackcap was born in the previous calender year – it has just successfully completed its first annual migration. But what I am particularly intrigued by is the "with pollen" business; it is a term I have not heard before. When this bird is processed, and the others in the team are out checking the nets again, I ask what it means.

Recent recoveries of blackcaps wearing rings have shown that birds wintering in the British Isles are from a central European breeding population from Austria and southern Bavaria. The summer breeding population of blackcaps that are now returning to the British Isles will have spent the winter in the foothills of the Atlas mountains in Morocco, and the coastal hills of Algeria; although, from evidence of a Blackcap ringed at Beachy Head in November and found nine weeks later in Sénégal, it seems that some of them winter further south in West Africa.

On their northward migration in spring, blackcaps feed in the trees around the Mediterranean and as they forage a film of sticky resin and pollen dust begins to build up at the base of the bill and lower forehead, forming a crust. Some of this pollen has been analysed and turns out to be from *Citrus* species. If the birds are held up by bad weather for a long time the crust becomes bigger and bigger and is a good indicator of how long they have spent in that particular area. Recording details like the pollen crust are only possible by close examination of birds in the hand; again showing that bird ringing is vital to our understanding of many different aspects of a bird's life.

A male blackcap in the hand showing the pollen crust. The female blackcap has a rufous crown.

"Sometimes when it's a thick shield, it's a wonder how they can see," says Mick. I lean forward and take a closer look at the bird he is still holding. This early on in my journey it is an incredible feeling being so close to such tangible evidence of migration. Without reference to its weight or ring number I can see that only a matter of days, or perhaps a week or so ago, this tiny bird must have been almost 2000 kilometres south of Portland Bill.

Before the day is too far advanced I ought to take another turn around the Bill and see what else is about. Outside, the day has warmed and sunny pockets in the shelter of blackthorn and brambles are filled with oscillating columns of gnats; a chiffchaff is calling, and there are good numbers of redstarts about as well. The sea breeze is still sprinkled with swallows, but this time there are two house martins with them – the first I have seen this year.

From the shelter of the holiday huts and chalets that cover the ground below the observatory, I scan the commons again looking for the wheatears – they have all gone. Having travelled across the sea last night and made their landfall here at first light this morning, and after feeding and resting for a couple of hours, they have continued on their journey north. Tomorrow morning, if the weather stays the same, another wave will arrive soon after dawn. But, if in the days to come the pressure builds and the weather turns fine, there will be fewer birds to ring. Large numbers of migrants, with good visibility and travelling on light following winds, will then overfly the coast of southern Britain and make their first landfall much farther inland. I have been fairly lucky today.

As the year turns through spring towards early summer, the wintry circulation of weather patterns in the northern hemisphere steadily weakens and a gradually improving flow of anticyclones, ridges and warm

A sprinkling of yellow wagtails among sheep on the Ouse washes. Male yellow wagtails arrive back from Africa about two weeks earlier than the females.

fronts make their way into Europe. Anticyclonic weather is relatively inactive and often lingers for several days, sometimes spreading to join up with continental high pressure areas lying further east and south creating a huge fine weather window for migrants to make their way through with relative ease. The northward spring migration is further facilitated by settled weather and following warm winds which are generally associated with these 'highs'. It is not unusual for birds to overshoot their destination.

However, if spring migrants encounter really severe conditions, migration can be virtually halted and sometimes even reversed. But, a bird has no way of predicting what the weather conditions might be if it were to delay or speed up its journey. With the more urgent pace to the spring migration, northbound migrants must press on even though that might involve travelling when weather conditions are bad – conditions that during the more leisurely southward autumn migration would perhaps see the passage interrupted for a while.

Of the meteorological factors affecting bird movements, perhaps temperature is the most important. It effects the availability of the insect food on which many smaller migrants depend and food availability largely governs the rate of spread of the northward migration. Lengthening or shortening of daylength is important too, as it affects the time during which food is available.

Swallows advance over Europe at a relatively leisurely pace. From first reaching the southern extremes of the continent at the western end of the Mediterranean, it takes the vanguard an average of 109 days to reach northern Scandinavia. They must allow time for sufficient insects to rise into the airspace where they feed. Although the advance is slow at the beginning, and speeds up a little towards the end in the north, the rate of spread or 'advancing front' of swallows is reckoned to be about 40 km per day.

The advance of the willow warblers begins twenty days later than the swallow, and spreads at a rate of about 46 km per day. They have less need to delay their migration through southern Europe, because the shelter and relative warmth down among the leaves and breaking buds encourages an early growth of insects on which the warblers can feed.

The advancing front of swifts across Europe is even later and the pace is more rapid. Their arrival in temperate latitudes must be delayed until rising temperatures in late spring and early summer draw enough aerial plankton into the sky to sustain them.

But in general the spring migration is more hurried than autumn; its greater pace has advantages. By arriving early on the breeding grounds the birds have a longer time in which to breed and, with fewer birds to compete against, a favourable breeding territory is more easily secured. The main disadvantage is that a satisfactory food supply might not be available early in the season, and if sudden or prolonged cold weather were to prevent them from finding food, there would be a serious risk of starvation. The advantage then would be with the later arrivals that would turn up on the breeding grounds already in better condition.

During the winter months, and more so during the spring and autumn migration seasons, one of the most evocative ornithological images occurs where tides ebb and flow across wide expanses of tidal mud-flats and estuaries around the coastline of the British Isles and continental Europe. Tightly packed, sometimes in flocks of thousands, the concerted movements of waders rise and fall like smudges of smoke caught in the wind. Twisting and turning with remarkable synchronous agility they move between the tides, shuttling between the exposed mud of the feeding grounds and the dryer shingle banks, saltmarshes and beaches where they must wait in safety as the tide rises and covers their larder of food. If the swirling mass sweeps near enough the sound they make is equally exciting; the rush of air through two, three or four thousand pairs of wings and distinctive call-notes add to the spectacle.

The dunlin is the most common of small waders seen on the inter-tidal mudflats of Europe and three recognised geographical races occur regularly. Although there is some overlap between them, each race is distinguishable by certain plumage characteristics and measurements of bill-length and body size.

The 'Southern' dunlin *Calidris alpina schinzii* breeds in the British Isles,

Dunlin arriving at a roost on Morecambe Bay during the spring migration. Almost all the birds have attained their full summer plumage, most noticeably the distinctive black belly.

around the Jutland peninsula and the Baltic States, southern Scandinavia and Finland as well as Iceland, the Faeroes and a pocket in eastern Greenland. The bulk of these birds winter in north west and west Africa, particularly Morocco and the Banc d'Arguin in Mauritania. In western Europe they occur only in the migration seasons, on passage between the winter and summer quarters.

Schiøler's dunlin *C. a. arctica*, which breeds in north-east Greenland, also only occurs in Europe at migration time as it passes to and from its wintering grounds (these are not fully known, but ringing studies so indicated that they are mainly in north and west Africa).

The third race of dunlin is *C. a. alpina* or the 'Northern' dunlin which breeds in northern Scandinavia and Finland, Spitsbergen, then eastwards across northern USSR as far as the Kolyma River. This race is the abundant winter visitor to the mudflats and estuaries of western Europe, although some reach as far south as the Mediterranean with the coast of Morocco being their southern limit.

In mid-winter Britain and Ireland are home to about 500,000 dunlin which is about half the total population wintering in western Europe. Wintering with them are numerous other waders including about 40,000 grey plovers, huge numbers of sanderling, ringed plovers and turnstones, and over 300,000 knot.

What many of these long distances migrants have in common is a style of migration where they make long, non-stop flights between specific staging areas. Needing almost exclusively mud or soft ground to find their food they rely on a series of suitable estuaries and coastal wetlands with abundant and readily available food supply where they are able to feed and rest before continuing their journey. But suitable staging areas between the Arctic and Africa are scarce so waders have a tendency to follow fairly well-defined routes or 'flyways', regularly visiting the same traditional localities through the year – as moulting and wintering grounds, or as staging posts. This traditional use of staging areas is highlighted by one dunlin that in 1974, 1976 and 1980 was caught as it migrated up the west coast of the British Isles on the same day, of the same month, at exactly the same location every time.

British and Irish estuaries and those on the near continent in Holland and Germany are particularly important to wintering and passage waders in three ways. Firstly, the climate for these northern latitudes is relatively mild due to the warming effect of the Atlantic Gulf Stream. Secondly, there is also a large rise and fall in the tides which regularly exposes extensive feeding areas creating ideal conditions for waders that cannot cope with freezing conditions and which need large areas of soft mud. Thirdly, the estuaries are strategically placed, lying at the confluence of the East Atlantic Flyway (see map on page 39), a term that describes the mass of migratory paths of many different wader species as well as encompassing their summer and winter ranges.

Dunlin flock approaching a high tide roost on Morecambe Bay.

During the spring and autumn migration periods when there is overlap between large numbers of wintering and passage birds, the coastal wetlands of western Europe are of outstanding international importance. Bird ringing has shown that birds from as far away as Canada and Siberia travel the flyway using a large number of European intertidal mudflats and smaller coastal wetlands. As well as the waders there are the enormous numbers of wildfowl dependent on them too.

However, despite the ornithological significance of these vast muddy landscapes, they have been subject to many development ideas and proposals over the years. It is often suggested that these 'wasted spaces' would be better used for tidal power schemes, reservoirs for water storage, fisheries and leisure pursuits, or simply claimed for agriculture. All of these development proposals would have effects in varying degrees on the birds whose lives depend on these simple yet productive landscapes. The consequences for many thousands of birds of removing only one link in the chain of flyway estuaries would be extremely damaging.

To better safeguard coastal wetlands in the British Isles it was long ago realised that to support the conservation case estuarine bird populations must be continuously monitored and studied in depth. For the past 18 years the Birds of Estuaries Enquiry, organised by the BTO has involved a number of other conservation bodies and many voluntary participants. Also adding to the growing store of information have been wader study groups, who not only have been catching and marking birds on British and European estuaries, but groups of ringers have mounted expeditions to different locations on the flyway – from Greenland, Iceland and Norway to Mauritania and Morocco.

I cannot hope to fill in the complete picture of wader movements on the East Atlantic Flyway, but sketches from one location will colour in a little detail.

A few days previously I had phoned Jack Sheldon. "The Dunlin flock is at about twelve or fifteen thousand now", he said, continuing in a voice full of promise, "the weather looks fine this coming weekend and the tides are right. There's a good chance that we'll go for a catch, so it might be best to come up – the birds could be gone by the following weekend".

I took his advice. On Friday morning May 5th I am sitting with Jack and his wife Jane in the dining room of their house, drinking coffee, talking birds and looking out over what must be one of the best views from any birder's house in Britain. The house stands at the edge of rough grassy dunes facing the sea on the north end of Walney Island. The island itself is long and low lying, its southern tip curling gently into the mouth of Morecambe Bay, the largest west coast estuary and one of the most important for birds in the British Isles. Its saltmarshes, sand and shingle spits, and vast inter-tidal mudflats, are a vital link to many thousands of waders travelling the flyway.

The return passage eastwards of the *alpina* birds that have wintered here begins as early as February and continues into early April. At the same time

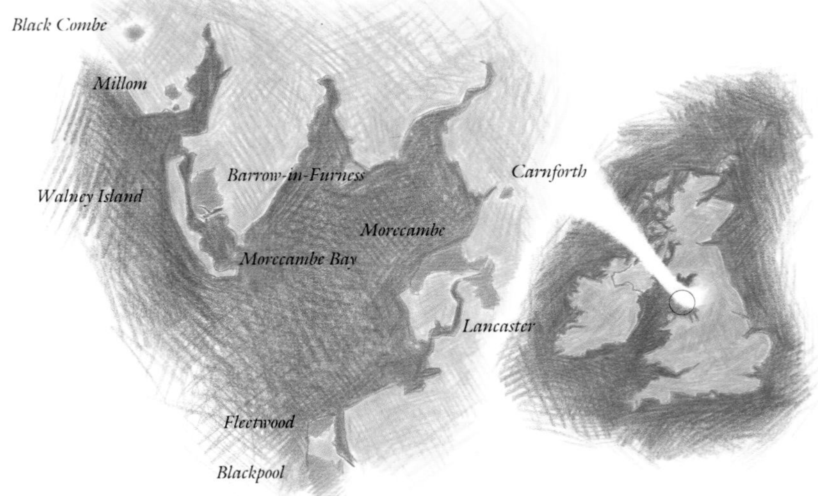

they are largely replaced by *schinzii* birds travelling from Africa and bound for Iceland.

Here at Morecambe Bay many dunlin break their northward journey for three or four weeks. They feed busily to build up their reserves of 'fuel' which is stored as body fat. It is this fuel that will see them through the next stage of their journey.

Each day brings more and more birds – a few days ago the Dunlin flock gathered at one high tide roost on Walney was about 2000 birds – it is now between 10,000 and 15,000. When conditions are right, sometime between the very end of April and early May, they leave for the north. Sometimes they briefly stop once more in the western isles of Scotland, or if the winds are favourable and the pressure high, they cross the North Atlantic direct to Iceland.

"They wait until almost high tide", says Jack, "the whole flock flying about calling and circling, and gaining height slowly. Then a portion break off and flying upwards at about 45° head north-northwest, just to the left of Black Combe". He turns and points out of the window towards the distant hill looming hazily in the bright morning sunshine. "Away they go, it's a wonderful sight like". I bet it is!

High tide tomorrow will be just after one o'clock in the afternoon and that is when Jack and his team from the Morecambe Bay Wader Group plan to catch the birds. Between now and then there is a lot to be done; sorting and loading of equipment, telephoning to make sure a full complement of members can make it for the weekend. He also takes me out to check the high tide roost, the site the birds have been using for the past week or so – fortunately all looks well.

Today is catching day and it is fine and clear with a light breeze coming in across the bay from the south-west. The short cropped grassy swards on the southern end of the island are littered with debris carried in on the highest tides. The light southerly winds also brought in some wheatears last night. A count of seven, eight or nine birds at a time reveals only one or two

Observations of Dunlin coming into roost. The characteristic simultaneous concerted turns and changing colours of thousands of dunlin in flight are eye-catching, but extremely difficult to capture on paper.

males. Four weeks ago at Portland Bill it was the males that were the most numerous as they passed through in advance of the females.

On the damper saltmarsh there are whimbrel and shelduck with thin clouds of swallows and sand martins sweeping through the sea-breeze above. Then high up, far out over the sea, a lone swift is heading inland – a first for the year.

The catching site is a short stretch of bouldered and coarse pebbled beach that remains dry when the tide peaks. Setting the nets is a painstaking business because the type they will be using are cannon nets. Explosive charges in two mortar-like barrels fire projectiles attached by short ropes to lightweight nets measuring about 30 by 15 metres. The launch is almost instantaneous and the nets reach their full extent and descend on the roosting birds before even a wing is raised in an effort to escape. On average a wader catch with a cannon net might be about 200 or so, but there was once a catch of over 3000 birds.

Two nets are laid out along the top edge of the beach parallel to the incoming tide then furled into narrow, shallow trenches. A third 'back-up' half-net is set at right angles to the others, and that too is furled into a trench. When the nets are set and the beach in front of them cleared of any dangerous debris, command wires are fed back to a sandy hollow well back from the beach where the group have made a base. A couple of hours before high tide, everything is ready. Out over the estuary, where all but the highest mud and shingle banks are covered by the sea, there are wader flocks on the move – passing waves of oystercatchers, loose bunches of turnstones and the huge swirling flocks of dunlin. As the tide finally fills the estuary and begins to climb the shingle spits and scars below us on the beach, the dunlin begin to gather in larger and larger numbers on the roost close to the nets, the flashing white and soft warm browns of their plumage in flight suddenly vanishing as they land in a sprinkle along the pebbly shore. Through the telescope I watch them face the wind and begin preening or simply resting by turning to push their forehead and bill into the feathers on their backs. Then suddenly for some unseen reason they are all up in the air again sweeping around the roost site calling. Then, just as quickly, they land back on the beach again.

During all this time, Jack's team are waiting – reminiscing over past catches and talking hopefully about what today's outcome could be. Some of them have travelled 100 miles or more to be here. All eyes are on the swirling flocks, but they look inland occasionally too, on the watch for straying walkers and their dogs – many a catch has been lost from disturbance by wandering pets.

High tide passes and the number of birds peaks, but the 'centre of gravity'

The dark bellies and lighter flanks and upper parts of the dunlin reflect similar contrasts in light and shade of the rocks and pebbles on the shore.

Removing the catch from the nets. Once extracted the birds are placed in special boxes ready for moving up the beach to the ringing site.

of the roost is beyond the reach of the nets. Watching from a distance Jack speaks into his two-way radio, "David, are you there?"

"Yes."

"There's a lot of birds in the hollow to your left…it might be best now to try working your way up towards us."

"OK."

For the past half hour I have been concentrating on the birds and had not noticed where David was, but now I can just see him lying face down on the beach on the far side of the birds. Crawling inch by inch towards them, his slow manoeuvrings controlled by radio contact with Jack who has sole responsibility for the firing. Jack has taken up a position which gives a good view down the line of the nets. A third radio back at the team's base behind the beach keeps the rest of the team fully informed and alert. Gently the bulk of the roosting Dunlin are moved towards the reach of the nets. David's object is not to disturb the whole flock but to persuade those birds nearest to him to lift and move to the other end of the roost. Cautious and patient movements like this, in ringers jargon known as 'twinkling', can move a flock 100 or 200 metres along a beach. Jack's experience over the years has taught him that successful 'twinkling' is best achieved when the roost has been established for some time as the birds are then less likely to leave for an alternative roosting site. David Norman is clearly a good 'twinkler'.

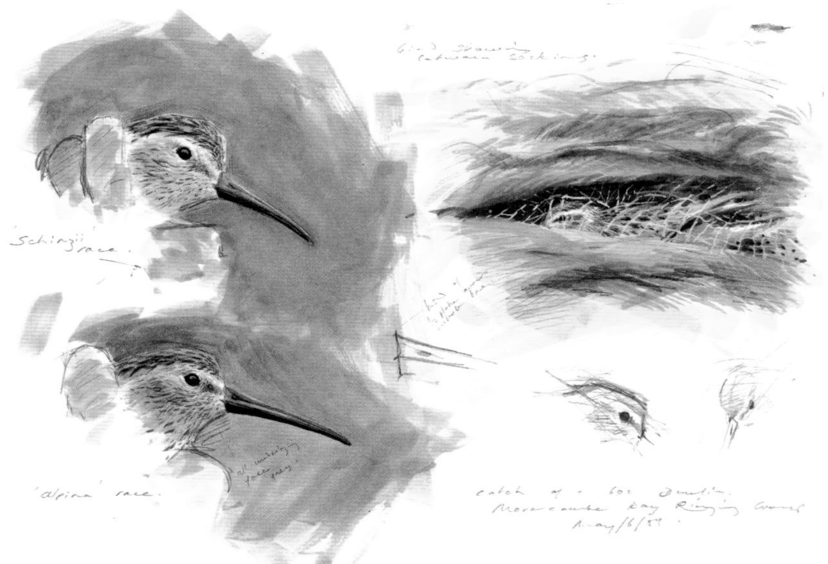

A sample of the catch showing a schinzii *(top left) and an* alpina *dunlin.*

Another five minutes, "Hold it, David". The last 'twinkle' has moved another 700 or so dunlin towards the nets and there are a good number now within catching distance. Jack judges the situation carefully but quickly – the flock could move off at any moment and the chance to fire would be gone. When the last bird has settled. Jack speaks quietly into his radio, "That's it, we're going to fire". A few seconds later, at just after twenty past one, comes the deep thud as the cannons go off. The air is filled with the roar of the thousands of birds the nets have missed taking off and the rattle of pebbles as the ringing group race from cover down the beach, each person carrying a bundle of sacking towards nets trembling with the strain of caught birds. As quickly as they can the team spread the sacking over the trapped birds: under cover they will quickly quieten down. When that is done, special boxes to carry the birds back up the beach are fetched and the careful work of extracting them from the nets begins.

The previous few catches had been low in numbers so there's an air of excitement about this one – obviously it is large.

"How many?" I ask Jack.

"About five or six hundred, I reckon", he replies.

As the nets are cleared the birds are moved back up the beach to where the processing of the catch will be done and there they are canopied under more sacking to diffuse the heat of the sun. As part of the team set about clearing the beach of nets and equipment, the others split into three processing teams and spread themselves out in the grass. Watching from a distance the ringing site has the air of a bustling nomad encampment. Closer in I sit sketching and listening.

"Here's a bird you missed – it's a Reykjavik."

"Ring number 79 is a juvenile *alpina*."

"Whose doing controls?"

"80 is a male *schinzii*."

"Weight 49."

Some of these dunlin are relatively light and therefore must have arrived on Morecambe Bay fairly recently. Other birds have been here longer and have had more time to put on weight, in the form of energy rich fat, prior to departure for Iceland. After a long journey a dunlin will have used up most of its energy stores and its weight would be about 36 or 38 grammes, but immediately before departing on a long journey it should have increased its weight to about 70 or 80 grammes.

By late afternoon the processing of the catch is complete and the mass of raw data logged on paper. The total catch is 670 birds – all of them Dunlin. Two thirds of the birds are *schinzii*, one third *alpina* and only one or two *arctica*. There are 10 're-traps' of birds caught and ringed before at Walney Island and there are 15 'controls' of birds bearing rings from other catching sites – a bird caught last year in Poole Harbour, others caught two years ago at Teesmouth, in Dublin Bay three years ago and one from the coast of Dumfries and Galloway caught four years ago, as well as two bearing Icelandic rings, two French, and one Portugese.

For the moment, the exact history and previous whereabouts of these 'foreign birds' is unknown, but in time when the details emerge, more links in the migratory chain on the East Atlantic Flyway can be put in place.

Although not as spectacular as thousands of waders on the move, there are aspects of the migration story in almost every corner of the landscape so I am keeping an extra careful watch on my 'local patch' just outside the village – a place where I go as often as I can. It is a small mosaic of meadows, thick hedges, ponds, spinneys and a tiny wood surrounded by huge expanses of intensive agriculture.

It is the kind of East Anglian landscape that for much of the year is sprinkled with birds like partridges, rooks, crows and pheasants. Wrens rattle away deep in hedges, and there are always dunnocks, blackbirds and robins. A pair of kestrels breed close by and this year a pair of little owls have moved into an old tree stump in a hedge. Autumn brings not only redwings and fieldfares but also surprises; last autumn five whimbrel flew over and if they had not called when directly overhead, I would never have known they had passed.

In summer the area fills with migrants. Cuckoos come and there are whitethroats, willow warblers, blackcaps and chiffchaffs too. I have seen sedge warblers passing through but never staying, and I startled a redstart out of the hedge as I walked along.

Since returning from Morecambe Bay four days ago the weather has been the same – continuous high pressure and nothing but clear skies and light southerly breezes and it has been warm. Looking at the weather map of Europe this morning, May 10th, a complex pattern of high pressure areas spread virtually from North Africa to the Baltic. The outlook for the next 48 hours? – dry, bright and warm but with cloud and some light rain in the extreme north of the country. If ever weather conditions can be said to be ideal for northbound migrants, then this is it.

Hobby on the wing catching dragonflies.

Before going north when the weather was a little less settled, a walk round the patch by the usual route revealed a sprinkling of early migrants. I heard a whitethroat singing and here and there willow warblers threw their songs from the hedgerows. But the walk this evening reveals the arrival of many more migrants, most of them possibly taking advantage of the high pressure and favourable winds.

The lane up to the meadows is a bright alley speckled yellow with cowslips on the banks, and cluttered with the overhanging green and white of hawthorns still in flower. There are at least two whitethroats proclaiming territory now, and the first garden warbler of the year is singing at the top end of one meadow. There are more blackcaps as well, and a pair of turtle doves lingering in the willows in the wet corner of other meadow.

The sun is getting low as I retrace my steps down the lane and where it meets the road again I bear right and head up a grassy track. High above bundles of swifts scream against a background of massive cloud stacks tinged with soft orange evening light. In a field entrance at the top end I set up my telescope and stool and sit down to wait and see whether one very special migrant is back.

Looking towards one particular and very familiar tree, I scan the cluster of dead branches jutting from the top – nothing. I scan left to the tall stump of an ash tree further down the field edge, and there it is – the hobby is back! For half-an-hour, until it is almost dark, I sit watching the beautiful falcon preening – pulling at its long flight feathers, then turning and twisting to work through its tail and breast feathers.

During their summer stay here, hobbies lead a very secluded existence and so they are difficult to record, but the UK breeding population is estimated to be well over 300 pairs. As well as weather and other natural hazards, it is people that pose the greatest threat to the breeding attempts of any rare bird, and the hobby in the British Isles is certainly a rare breeding bird. So, from this same safe distance I will check this site again over the next few days, then leave it alone until later in the summer.

When the adult birds are out hunting food for the young I will come up here sometimes and watch them; or if I am very lucky, I might see one of them from the studio window as I have done in summers past.

The return each year of ones 'own' migrants always has a special significance; the swallows in the barn, the house martins under the eaves, or Swifts in the roof; or in the case of somebody who phones me up each year to announce proudly, 'My spotted flycatchers are back'.

It is incredible to think that since last September 'my' Hobbies have travelled many thousands of kilometres into the heart of Africa. It is even more extraordinary to think that they will have made that journey many times before. For the past four years to my knowledge they have returned, within a margin of only a few days in early May, and they or their young return to the same nest in the same tree in the same corner of the English landscape.

CHAPTER THREE

Northwards to the Arctic

The East Atlantic Flyway, the term used to describe the mass of migratory paths of many different species, as well as their summer and winter ranges.

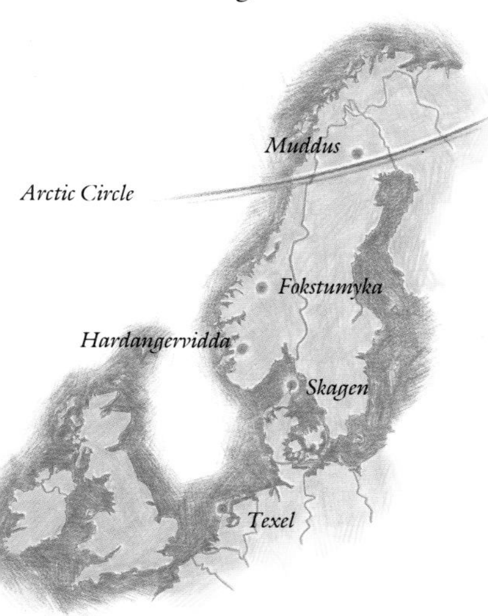

The migratory pathways that birds follow as they come and go with the seasons can be indicated easily enough by drawing lines and arrows on a map. From the results of ringing studies, radar and direct field observations conducted over many years there is enough information to map some of those arrows with considerable accuracy.

However, these diagrams of migration must necessarily be over-simplifications as they cannot hope to represent the seasonal movements of either an individual bird, or of a whole population of perhaps many millions. All they can do is indicate the general direction and overall pattern of movements of a species or a population within it. Marking a migratory feature like the East Atlantic Flyway on a map is an even broader generalisation because that attempts to define a distinguishable pattern of migration routes which are used by whole groups of related species.

A way of trying to unravel one small part of this enormous migratory tangle, is to find a pathway of my own and journey north through Europe, and on to the arctic. By staying broadly within the bounds of the East Atlantic Flyway and stopping here and there in a few chosen landscapes, I can look for species in the field that might help explain some of those arrows on the theoretical map of migration.

Texel is the first in a chain of islands which curve around the North Sea coasts of the Netherlands, West Germany and south-west Jutland as far as Esbjerg in Denmark. The islands enclose extensive areas of shallow water that strung together form one of the most important inter-tidal wetlands on the East Atlantic Flyway – the Waddensee. The Dutch Waddensee alone supports up to one and a half million moulting, wintering or migrating waders, as well as many thousands of wildfowl.

Ten days have passed since I saw the hobby return to its old site near my home. Now, in mid-morning on a fine clear day towards the middle of May, I am sitting high up on the sea-wall overlooking the Schorren, a promontory of muddy saltmarsh built up where two passing currents meet and drop their silt on the north-east side of Texel. At high tide the Schorren is a roosting site for many thousands of birds.

Vlieland, the next island in the chain shimmers in the distance, trembling in the heat haze hanging over the vast muddy expanse of the Waddensee exposed by the retreating tide. Spread across the mudflats and tidal pools, as far as the eye can see, is the movement of many hundreds of feeding birds.

Studies of three bar-tailed godwits feeding in a meadow on Texel. Before the start of the breeding season bar-tailed godwits undergo a partial moult involving some, but not all of the body feathers. This partial pre-breeding moult happens any time from late February to May, but mostly in April. It is, in a sense, a 'smartening up' of the plumage in readiness for the forthcoming breeding season.

As the hours pass and the tide begins to flow back again the pace of activity among the birds quickens as they begin to be pushed from their feeding grounds by the rising tide. Grainy clusters of knot and tighter wisps of dunlin, small flocks of ringed plovers, straggling lines of oystercatchers and turnstones start weaving their distinctive patterns across the sky and mud. Bar-tailed godwits, grey plovers, redshank and curlew are on the move as well; gradually the Schorren starts to fill with birds.

As the tide rises higher the brent geese out on the mudflats lift-off in ever increasing numbers and start pouring over the sea-wall in loose straggling flocks, dropping down towards their refuge on the Polder de Eendracht, just inland from the Schorren. An hour before high tide the roosting geese are packed onto the short turf like office workers in a city park on a hot summer lunchtime. From the middle to the end of May the number of brent geese on Texel reaches a peak of about 7500 birds.

Like many long-distance migrant wader species, migrating geese rely on a series of traditional staging areas where they can break the journey and refuel. On the southward migration these brent geese, like most migratory geese populations, had major staging areas only a relatively short distance south of the breeding range. This meant that, soon after the energy sapping summer tasks of raising young and moulting were over, the adult birds could recover lost weight and condition in preparation for the long onward journey to western Europe. The young birds will also have had a little longer to grow before attempting their first long-distance migration.

KNOT, TEXEL

Studies of two knot and quicker sketches of a bar-tailed godwit and two avocets. The knot, or red knot *Calidris canutus*, is the second largest of the Calidrid waders, the group that includes the stints, sandpipers, dunlin and sanderling. The largest is the great knot.

As a breeding species, the four races of knot are confined mostly to areas of moist tundra and glacial gravel on the peninsulas and islands of the remote high arctic. Outside the breeding season it is characteristically a gregarious bird of open coastal mudflats and estuaries where they sometimes gather in huge numbers.

As a classic long-distance migrant the knot utilises a number of estuaries as staging areas and makes just a few long non-stop flights between them.

Only two of the four races of knot *C. c. canutus* and *C. c. islandica* are regular and abundant travellers on the East Atlantic Flyway. The *canutus* breeding birds from north central Siberia are chiefly passage migrants to western Europe, moving through rapidly to moulting and wintering areas on the Atlantic coasts of Africa, from Morocco south to Mauritania. Some reach South Africa.

The *islandica* breeding birds from northern Greenland and north-east Canada winter mostly around the coasts of the southern North Sea south to western France. This Atlantic Europe population totals about 260,000 birds in mid-winter.

Through the course of the winter Knot move both between estuaries and between the British Isles and the continent. By early spring most have congregated at a very few estuarine staging areas, principally in the Irish Sea basin, and the Wash and the Waddensee areas around the North Sea. At these locations in March and April they put on weight in readiness for the long journey ahead. By the beginning of May, fully refuelled, they are on migration back to their breeding grounds.

However, the familiar staging areas on the arctic coast that the geese used on the way south are still frozen over in early May, but still the birds must put on weight and partially moult in anticipation of the coming journey and summer breeding season. So they pause much further back down the flyway, on the Waddensee, where many often remain until well into May.

When the time is right and the weather favourable they leave to make a long non-stop flight to the north coast of the USSR then eastwards to reach their high arctic breeding grounds early in June.

As the tide turns in early afternoon a marsh harrier appears high over the polders and drifts out towards the wader roost. As it passes over the geese their heads come up and a noisy wave of unease passes through them. When the harrier approaches the waders it has a greater effect; godwits, plovers, dunlin, knot and avocets start lifting off and the air is soon filled with a mass of swirling birds. When the danger has passed the roost settles to resume the wait for the tide to fall.

When the sea-breeze dies away for a minute or two the sound of the birds are sharpened. The 'snipping' of meadow pipits on the sea-wall, a few inconspicuous phrases from a yellow wagtail down on the saltings, the metallic piping of oystercatchers and different sounds of other waders on the roost, and in the background the constant subdued chatter of seven and a half thousand geese – it is an exciting sight and sound.

Waders assembling at De Schorren on Texel. In late May the number of birds is at its peak: over 20,000 bar-tailed godwits, 15,000 knot, over 8000 dunlin and about 1500 grey plovers gather in readiness for the flight north.

In a while the shallow channels begin to drain and sticky margins once more appear along the edge of the saltings. Already there are waders on the move, dispersing to favoured feeding grounds. The brent geese, however, must wait a little longer for the tide to uncover the lower banks of green algae where they will feed until moved on by the tide again.

The west coast of the Jutland peninsula, as far as Esbjerg in Denmark, is topographically similar to the North Sea coasts of Germany and Holland, but from Esbjerg northwards it changes. In former times huge shallow inlets along this stretch of the coast were open to the sea, but sand-bars have grown to block the entrances, trapping large areas of open water, reeds, brackish marsh and wet meadows. These wetlands are home to many thousands of wintering wildfowl and a temporary resting place for countless thousands more waders and wildfowl travelling the East Atlantic Flyway.

It is mid-May when I reach the area of Nissum and Ringskøping Fjord. The shoreline and lagoons in the saltings are busy with avocets, redshank, grey plovers, oystercatchers and gull-billed terns. In the dunes and scrubby vegetation in the hollows are skylarks and crested larks, swallows, redstarts and whinchats, wheatears and a passing Montagu's harrier. Behind the dunes on the wet meadows are ruff, lapwing, common and wood sand-

A grey plover, most probably a female. When in breeding plumage the female has a brownish tinge to the underparts, and many whitish feathers; the male has almost solid black underparts.

The bean and brent geese of Nissum Fjord.

pipers, shelduck, wigeon and garganey. But it is the mix of geese which is interesting.

Among a small gathering of bean geese are four or five brent geese of the light-bellied race. The bean geese are a fragment of the much larger population that will have wintered mostly in the Baltic and North Sea regions of Europe, although small numbers will have reached as far south as Spain. The breeding range of bean geese is in the tundra and boreal zones across the entire Eurasian continent, but there is little evidence from ringing studies to link the different breeding populations to particular wintering areas. These birds will soon be leaving for breeding grounds in northern Scandinavia and Finland, or possibly even the western edge of the Soviet arctic and subarctic. However, where the brent geese are heading for is far more certain – their light bellies identify them as birds bound for the Svalbard archipelago of Greenland or the Franz Josef Islands.

The pink-footed geese gathered in the area tell a different story. They will have arrived here from their breeding grounds in the Svalbard archipelago in late September and early October last year. Before long almost the entire Svalbard population of between 12,000 and 15,000 birds will have gathered in the wetlands of west Jutland. But the autumn concentration will have been brief. More and more birds will have moved south to winter quarters in the coastal wetlands of the West Germany and the Netherlands. In late January the return migration will have begun, with numbers around Vest Stadil Fjord building up steadily through March and April. By now, however, many have stopped here to feed and then moved on. Soon it will be the turn of the few remaining birds to head north for the summer.

Large broad-winged birds, because of their weight and the energy requirements necessary to keep going over long distances using sustained flapping flight (high body weight to wing area ratio), rely on updraughts and rising warm air currents, or thermals, to help keep them aloft. Thermals rise from ground heated unevenly during the day by the sun and updraughts come from wind deflected by hills, tall buildings and sometimes even trees. The passage of larger birds on migration is facilitated by soaring high in one thermal then gliding down over considerable distances before rising up high again in the next. This 'thermalling' technique enables them to cover great distances with maximum efficiency, vital for long distance migration. However, thermals do not form over open water so soaring migrants must actively seek the shortest possible sea-crossings on their journey. This means that at peak migration times streams of birds are 'steered' around barriers of water and concentrated by geographical features like the narrows at Falsterbo in Sweden, the Straights of Gibraltar, the Bosphorus, the Bab-el-Mendeb straights between the Arabian peninsula and Africa, Kafer Kessem in Israel

A male Montagu's harrier. There are only between 40 and 50 pairs breeding in Denmark.

Raptor migration seen from Flagbakken with a particularly good passage of sparrowhawks.

and other locations that funnel birds in their hundreds of thousands as they journey between their breeding grounds and their wintering grounds.

Just short of Jutland's northern tip lies the hill of Flagbakken, a huge dome of sand rising above the surrounding pine covered dunes. For birds of prey making their way back to Scandinavia, the turbulence the hill creates and the thermals rising above the ancient dune system provides the final lift for birds heading off across the sea towards Sweden – it is a great place to watch the migration of soraing birds.

In the early afternoon, with light north-easterly winds, a steady passage of raptors drifts north. Buzzards are quite numerous and there are a few rough-legged and honey buzzards too. Large numbers of sparrowhawks and an occasional hobby pass through. The biggest surprise is a steppe eagle, but I worry about my identification. That is, until the following day when a keen Dutch 'twitcher' (jargon for a fanatical bird watcher) appears on the hill and tells me that a steppe eagle has been seen in the area over the past two days. The northern tip of Jutland at migration times, like many other European coastal promontories, regularly produces birds that are way beyond their normal distribution or migratory range; steppe eagles breed from the Black Sea eastwards, and migrate to winter quarters in Africa.

A few kilometres north of Flagbakken the coastal dune system finally runs out. Just past the lighthouse at Skagen the ancient sand accumulations reach

A hobby heading north across the Skagerraks towards southern Scandinavia. Although they sometimes soar, slim-winged and fast-flying birds of prey, like the hobby, do not have to rely on thermals to make their journey.

a slender peninsula of curling spits and sand bars that point north-east towards Sweden lying 60 km across the Skagerraks.

Early morning by the lighthouse sees skies overcast, but the cloud ceiling is high and the winds light so there should be some passage of small migrants to watch.

The huge spring passage of finches, thrushes and pipits, for which Skagen is noted, has past its peak now, but small numbers of meadow pipits and skylarks are on the move. I hear a few yellow wagtails passing high overhead, and not long after the rattling call of a handful of fieldfares moving down a wooded hollow in the dunes behind me. Through the morning swallows pass in an almost continuous flow of ones and twos with every now and then the passage of twenty or thirty in a shower. For some of these large groups I lay my compass on a page in the sketch pad, following them by sight for as long as I can as they head out to sea, all the while checking their compass heading and recording it with a quick line on the paper. Not very scientific but after the passage of a few flocks the marks are clustered roughly around a north-east heading, the direction of the shortest sea-crossing between northern Europe and Scandinavia.

Hardangervidda in southern Norway is a massive plateau at the southern end of the Scandinavian mountain chain. The mountains are a climatic boundary between the influence of the oceanic climate in the west that brings cool damp summers, and the bitterly cold winters of the continental climate in the east. In the Scandinavian mountains birch marks the upper tree line. On the higher and dryer slopes it forms scant and stunted cover, but on sheltered slopes and in valleys it forms into a more luxuriant meadow birch forest with marshland and bogs filling the valleys and hollows.

Much of Hardangervidda lies above the tree-line, so it is rich in arctic and subarctic flora – purple saxifrage, burberry and crowberry, bird's-eye primrose and mountain avens. As if to emphasise the arctic feel of this landscape, Europe's largest herd of reindeer live up here. Many of the birds, such as shore larks and Lapland buntings, Temminck's stints and purple sandpipers, are also typical of more northerly latitudes. Although the area is the most southerly outpost of arctic flora and fauna in Europe, bird species typical of temperate Europe also breed here, like cuckoos and wheatears, willow warblers and bluethroats. Up here on the great back of Hardangervidda in the second half of June there is a great mix of seasons, landscapes and birds.

Winter's snows have only half melted, but in sheltered pockets out of the wind the warmth of a bright clear early afternoon is working at what remains. The sound of running water fills every corner of the landscape: hidden streams run under collapsing bridges of ice and slush; overhanging tongues of ice drip peaty meltwater into dark pools; broad bouldered streams in full flood tumble between banks of drifted snow. The small lakes and ponds have only patches of open water and some are still covered completely with greyish slush tinged turquoise with underlying ice. On the slopes, in warm pockets cleared of snow, are the glowing yellows of bird's-eye primrose and catkins of dwarf willow. Spring has so far only come in patches and summer will come late to this southern extension of the Arctic.

I can hear the mewing cry of golden plover and meadow pipits calling, then high above an area of boggy melt water pools a dunlin starts singing and displaying. For the past few months I have been encountering dunlin in their hundreds, sometimes thousands, as they flocked on their wintering grounds and northbound on migration. It is strange to be watching and listening to only one bird behaving so differently – hovering against the wind, quivering and arching its wings, at the same time pouring out a long drawn-out liquid trill. After a long migration, for one dunlin at least it is clearly journey's end.

From under a boulder a small bird suddenly dashes out, but I soon lose sight of it. But after careful searching I find a nest tucked deep down in amongst the woody stems of crowberry and half-buried in peat. It is lined with moss and lichen with four greyish brown, almost dark olive eggs speckled with brown and black. As I move away and take cover a male Lapland Bunting appears and soon after the less strikingly marked female returns to the nest. These small seed-eating birds are summer migrants to breeding haunts in the alpine and arctic zones of northern Europe and eastwards across the USSR. Most head south-east and make for south central

Asia for the winter. But every year a fair sprinkling drift westwards and can be found around the southern shores of the North Sea.

There are shore larks up here as well. I watch a pair chasing each other from tussock to tussock, calling frequently with a short and repeated jingling phrase. Shore larks are migrants too, travelling to the coasts of countries around the southern North Sea and western Baltic regions, with a few reaching the shores of eastern Britain virtually every year.

Away from the mountains and travelling north again, the landscape now becomes almost continuous conifer forest; the edge of the great Eurasian taiga. In northern Sweden where the taiga has its westernmost outpost, the expanse of conifers is fragmented by a rich mosaic of swamps, lakes and peaty tarns with 'islands' of gravel and stone covered with dryer heath vegetation and virgin pine and spruce woods. These swamp-woods are a characteristic element of the northern Fenno-Scandian landscape. Breeding in this mosaic of arctic habitats are hazel grouse, rustic buntings, rough-legged buzzards, pine grosbeak and hawk owls, which are joined for the summer by migrants travelling from winter quarters in southern Europe and Africa – whimbrel and wood sandpipers, swallows and swifts, willow and garden warblers, chiffchaffs, cuckoos and spotted flycatchers.

A male Lapland bunting displaying to a female on Hardangervidda.

THE YELLOW WAGTAIL COMPLEX

Studies of male yellow wagtails encountered in Scandinavia. The bottom left bird is a blue-headed bird from southern Sweden. The bottom centre and bottom right birds are from further north in Scandinavia and are either grey-headed birds with a hint of blue-headed, or blue-headed with a hint of grey-headed!

The yellow wagtail is a bird of vast complexity and morphology exhibiting fascinating and puzzling variations that are directly linked to geographical distribution. Different geographical races show obvious differences in the head colour of adult males in breeding plumage. There are now generally reckoned to be three yellow-headed races and 15 either grey, blue or black-headed races. But with overlapping geographical breeding ranges between both complexes and races, there are zones of hybridisation producing birds which have a classic 'field-guide' colouring of one race, but which show a hint of another. The racial identification of female yellow wagtails in summer plumage is even more difficult than males; the differences are so slight that they are almost impossible to detect and judge quickly in the field. Confirmation is best made by reference to the male of the pair, but confusion with other species and doubts in racial identification are always possible.

It is midnight on mid-summer's day in the Muddus National Park, north of the Arctic Circle. Under a thick blanket of cold damp cloud the light dims a little and the temperature drops, and in the twilight world of the short arctic 'night' the birds fall silent for an hour or two – but the silence is not absolute. In the early hours the melodic bugling call of a whooper swan echoes across the stillness and soon after a noisy party of Siberian tits moves through the trees behind me. 'Dawn' is signalled by the sudden noisy churring of a flock of Siberian jays come to see what I am doing.

After a late morning warm-up and refreshment in the van I head out again into the wilderness of peat and forest under skies still overcast and

A mosaic of forest and bog in the Muddus National Park north of the Arctic Circle.

damp. With the weather as it is swifts have been forced to feed low down and they are hurtling through the plagues of mosquitoes swarming over the quagmire; there are sand martins with them as well. A female yellow wagtail is busy snatching insects from moss banks and sedgy tussocks and accumulating a bundle in its bill ready for young in a nest somewhere nearby. It is not until I see the male that I confirm them as grey-headed or *thunbergi* birds.

I follow a meandering line of raised hummocks thickly covered with dwarf willow and creeping bilberry towards a pine wooded 'island'. Half way across a short clear piping call starts up just ahead of me and moments later a spotted redshank takes to the air calling more anxiously and a little shriller; it will have a nest or young close by. Backing off I quickly find a place to settle and watch. In a while the adult lands and every now and then I catch a glimpse of a downy chick stumbling lightly through the dense vegetation after its parent.

I remember a spotted redshank that I saw on the Ouse or Hundred Foot Washes in the fens of East Anglia as it headed north nine weeks ago. It was only a part of the way through its moult and had not acquired the full breeding plumage like this one, which is absolutely beautiful. They are elegant birds slightly larger but more slimly built than a redshank, they are longer legged and have a relatively longer bill as well. On males, like this one, the dark sooty blue-black feathers on the back and sides are speckled white; the female colouring is less intensive. The behaviour of this bird also gives a clue to its sex. In early or mid-June, not long after egg-laying, the females will have gathered into small flocks and left the breeding grounds, leaving the males to incubate the eggs and

raise the young. Males and juveniles will begin their southward migration in the second half of July and August.

There are other waders out here as well. Wood sandpipers and whimbrel mark my progress across the bog as they move between precarious holds on the top of small birches and sapling spruce calling all the while as I pass through their territories. Along the wet fringe of a pine wooded mound a snipe suddenly hurtles into the air a few metres in front of me. Its rise is not familiar, its slower and there is a large flash of white on the outside edges of the tail – it is a great snipe.

Along the edge of the pines a spotted flycatcher hawks insects and a tree pipit is displaying, its song is sharp and clear in the still damp air; a cuckoo calls, there is a whinchat singing, and above them all drifts a rough-legged buzzard searching the quagmire for voles.

At these latitudes the virgin pine forests are as equally atmospheric and exciting as the quaking bogs. The forest floor is bright with the orange and green mosses and lichens draped like a thick blanket over underlying contours of fallen trees, boulders and gravel mounds. Long shreds of dark grey-

A singing male wheatear in Scandinavia. Wheatears, continuously finding new breeding areas along the northern edge of their range as the last ice age ended, were able to increase their range fractionally year by year. In time they spread further and further eastwards across Eurasia into Alaska, and westwards into Greenland and eastern Canada as the ice retreated. But every autumn they returned via tried and tested but increasingly lengthy routes, to their traditional wintering grounds in Africa.

black lichen beards hang from tree limbs, and here and there are the huge domes of wood ant nests. The forest is noisy with bramblings, song thrushes and chaffinches singing and a black woodpecker passing through the tops of the trees gives a long liquid yelping call. There are siskins, as well as a pine grosbeak, and a hazel grouse hen clattering noisily through the undergrowth.

Although it is mid-summer, to my eye there is a permanent coldness locked into these northern swamps and forests on the taiga's edge. They have the look of landscapes left virtually untouched since they were formed in Europe's distant past, a look underlined earlier this morning when I watched a lone elk grazing the aquatic vegetation on a mire; there are still a few lynx, brown bears, wolverine and otters up here as well, further reminders of a wilder and more primaeval Europe.

About 1,500,000 years ago the present geological period, the Quaternary, began and since then there have been four major Ice Ages, each lasting 10,000 years or more and separated by long inter-glacial periods of equal duration. This long advance and retreat of the ice brought about an equally dynamic sequence of changes in the patterns of plant distribution. Each scouring action of the advancing ice sheets scraped away the habitats that had grown up in the intervening time, and landscapes not directly affected by the ice were changed by different climatic conditions advancing with the Ice Ages. This resulted in plants dying out along the northern edge of a habitat, as those at its southern edge spread. Thus, at the height of the last glaciation, the patterns of vegetation covering much of Eurasia differed greatly from those that we see today.

Immediately to the south of the ice sheets lay a broad band of treeless tundra and cold arctic steppes that stretched in a broad band from the Atlantic coast of western Europe across to Siberia and the Pacific Ocean in the east. Adjoining it to the south lay a waterlogged band of cold, lightly wooded and scrubby steppes, and further south still lay a mosaic of woodland and forested steppe reaching down to the mixed coniferous and broad-leaved forest surviving around the Mediterranean.

The vast expanse of open tundra and cold steppe lands would have provided a few bird species with ideal breeding habitats, so wheatears and red-throated pipits would have been far more numerous than they are today. But large numbers of other birds, many of them our familiar migrants, would have been greatly reduced or even eliminated from Europe by the lack of the right habitat. With virtually no woodland north of the Pyrénées, the Alps or the Black Sea, there would have been no willow warblers and no chiffchaffs, no redstarts or tree pipits, and severely reduced numbers of house and sand martins, spotted flycatchers, yellow wagtails and swifts. Grasshopper, sedge and reed warblers, common and lesser whitethroats would have survived in riverine and scrub vegetation.

The last Ice Age began to loosen its grip about 18,000 years ago. Over thousands of years, as summers lengthened and winters became less severe, the ice sheet retreated northwards. The broad belts of vegetation pushed south by severe climate and ice, were quick to follow the retreat. Arctic heaths colonised the bare and sodden glacier-carved landscape, then birch scrub crept over the arctic heaths. Warmer and drier conditions encouraged pine and small amounts of oak, hazel, elm and alder to spread north from their forest refuges in southern Europe. Over thousands of years each vegetation type crept northwards, occupying the climatic zone to which it was best suited.

As the boundaries of plant distribution changed, so did the distribution of birds, each species following the habitat it favoured. Redwings and fieldfares spread with birch scrub and arctic heaths. Willow warblers and tree pipits, redstarts and blackcaps, garden and wood warblers spread north with many other species from their scrub and woodland refuges around the Mediterranean and from further south in Africa.

In the summer the swallow, for example, existing successfully in warmer southern regions, would have been able to move beyond its normal range to feed in regions relatively free from competition. When the flush of insects waned in the autumn they could return south to warmer climates and ample feeding. The further north the swallow spread the further apart grew their two seasonal homes. As long as those making the annual journey were able to successfully raise more young than birds which stayed behind, and they and their offspring were able to accomplish the round-trip safely, then natural selection favoured the migrant. After a time, during which one part of the population would have been migratory and the other sedentary, the species as a whole becomes migratory.

If the changes wrought by the Ice Ages produced the migration patterns we see today, the origins of the migratory tendency in birds lies in the much more distant past.

Gradual changes in climate and vegetation on the drifting continental land-masses over 100 million years ago, when the ancestors of many present day bird species were evolving, would have stimulated early migrations. Like the relatively recent changes that birds have had to make as a result of the Ice Ages, ancient bird populations will have been forced to seek new habitats and the most favourable conditions. Over millions of years, the patterns of those movements would have changed many times as species evolved. Others, not quick enough to respond, would have died out. However, the most powerful agent, which finally fixed the migratory tendency in birds, was 'seasonality'. Seasonality is the flowering and fruiting of plants, or the sudden flush of insects after a period of rains, or the spawning of fish in a seasonal river, or any other predictable abundance which is a potential source of food. The existence of 'seasonality' would in turn have triggered bird populations into migrating in order to exploit the abundance. The Ice Ages, over a period of only a few thousand years, simply modified the distances the birds moved.

My journey northwards on the East Atlantic Flyway, from Morecambe Bay and Texel, has so far brought me 1,500 kilometres to northern Scandinavia and the western edge of the taiga. Beyond here 'at the end of the flyway' lies one more major vegetation zone – it is the tundra, an even

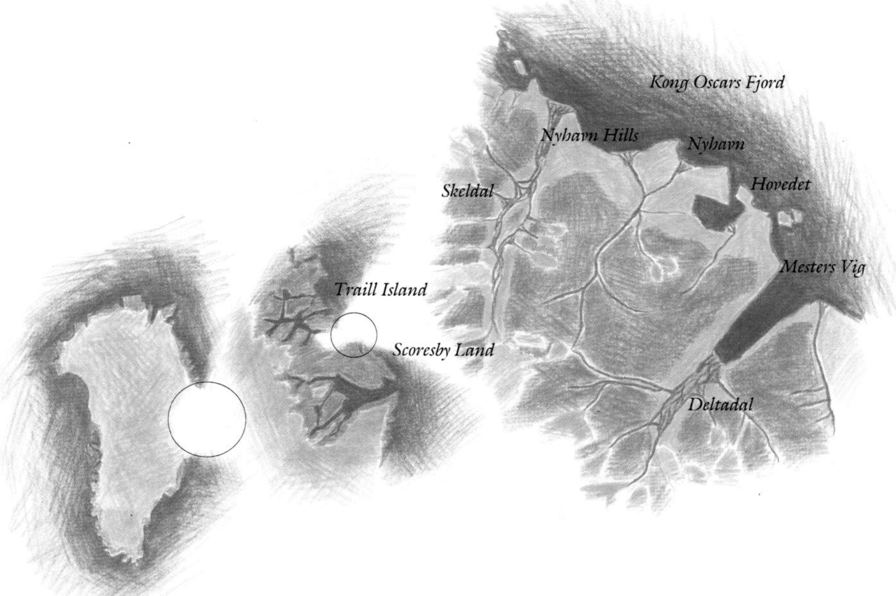

larger undisturbed reservoir of wilderness that for a few short months each summer is home for countless long-distance migrants .

The term tundra, derived from the Finnish word *tunturi,* meaning completely treeless heights, is often applied only to areas where the earth just below the surface lies permanently frozen, so called permafrost. It is more commonly applied to the vast areas of treeless landscape that stretches in a broad uneven ribbon around the arctic, between the taiga to the south and the Arctic Ocean to the north. In western Europe true tundra is confined to a narrow coastal strip in northern Scandinavia.

The tundra landscape is characterised by sparse vegetation, a ragged blanket of moss and lichen spread across ice-scoured valleys, bouldered hillsides, and arctic heaths, threaded by a mass of meltwater pools, bogs, lakes, rivers and streams. Tree growth – limited not only by the shortness of the growing season, but also by strong winds, underlying permafrost and poor quality soils – consists of dwarf birches and willows that creep along sheltered cracks and gulleys.

The climate during the short arctic summer can often be harsh and unpredictable, and the tundra can be a dangerous place for birds. Its remoteness will have more often than not involved them in a long and dangerous crossings of seas and icy wastes, and they will have used a lot of energy to reach it. But there are ecological factors that make going there advantageous for the species that do, and the chances of survival high enough to make it worth the risk.

One small tract of tundra wilderness which serves as a brief summer home to many migrants is Scoresby Land on the north-east coast of Greenland. Within this remote and dramatic high arctic landscape, at about 72°N, lies Mesters Vig, a complex of tundra habitats that rise in a narrow coastal

A party of barnacle geese on a tundra lake at Mesters Vig in north-east Greenland.

band from the shores of Kong Oscars Fjord to the foot of the Stauning Alps. Mesters Vig is my final destination at the northern end of the flyway.

Greenland is the largest island in the world and, although geographically part of North America and the Nearctic, it is linked to Eurasia by the seasonal flow of migratory birds. Covering the whole of its interior is a vast ice-cap which, although it has glaciers reaching the coast in places, is separated from the sea by a belt of mountainous land and a wilderness of alpine and tundra vegetation.

A few birds manage to survive during the 'dark time' of winter; ravens that scavenge the kills of polar bears and arctic foxes, and ptarmigan that feed where bitter winds sweep away the cover of snow. Then in very late April or early May, as the sun appears once more above the horizon, abrupt seasonal changes come to the tundra. The sea-ice loosens and the snow begins to melt. With increasing daylength plants begin to grow rapidly and there is a flush of invertebrate life. Arriving to take advantage of this sudden and brief summer abundance are large numbers of wildfowl and waders.

It is high summer in the Arctic and July is almost over. The sun has already begun its journey again down towards the total darkness of winter. The afternoon had been bright, clear and warm with virtually no wind at all. I have been working for most of the time in shirtsleeves, but as 'night' advanced it has grown increasingly colder. Now with the midnight sun just touching the far peaks of Traill Island and glinting on the interior ice-cap in the distance, I have had to put on every item of clothing I have got with me. Even though it is bitterly cold I have made a point of being out late to see the sun; the timelessness of permanent daylight adds profoundly to the sense of enormity of this cold high-arctic world.

I am high up among the boulders on the hillside of Hovedet, with Kong Oscars Fjord on one side and below me a plain of rolling arctic heath running down the coast for a kilometre or two. Across the stillness comes the creaking and groaning of drifting icebergs in the fjord – every now and then there is a thunderous crack and roaring splash as the large bergs topple and break up.

Out of sight around the back of the hill something disturbs a pair of long-tailed skuas and their calls continue for a long time until the danger passes. Eventually the empty silence is resumed. It is broken again by a party of Arctic terns arriving to feed in the shallows among the grounded icebergs below.

The Arctic tern is famous as a long-distance traveller and by general consent is considered to be THE migrant. They breed in colonies all around the shores of the Arctic, northern Atlantic and Pacific Oceans, but migrate to the other end of the world to 'winter' in Antarctic seas. The round-trip accomplished by many each year will be 30,000 kilometres or more – a journey that is unequalled by any other migrant.

I look up quickly when I hear the distant bark of a goose and scanning the open tundra below through the telescope soon locate the flock of barnacle geese. I count them, 28 adults and 35 goslings. It has been a good breeding season. They are spread out feeding on the tundra, each pausing briefly on a patch of vegetation then moving quickly to the next. The adult birds towards the outside edges of the grazing flock feed less voraciously and seem to pause longer with head up scanning for signs of danger. At this stage of their annual cycle barnacle geese, like other arctic breeding geese, are extremely vulnerable and looking closely at the birds it is possible to see why. The goslings show a mixture of downy feathers and well developed first juvenile plumage, but they still lack a full set of flight feathers. The adult birds are part-way through their moult and are also flightless. If danger threatens their only escape is to run for the safety of open water.

In this scene is the first indication of how productive the tundra environment is for geese, a group dependent solely on plant food. Not only are they able to maintain themselves and raise a brood, but also undergo a moult which consumes an additional 10% of their daily energy requirements. During the summer they are also able to lay down enough fat reserves to fuel the first major stages of the return migration. The reason they can satisfy these high energy demands are varied. Firstly, the food they eat is highly nutritious; after the dormancy of winter arctic plants are forced to grow fast in the short summer season and the growing tips are rich in protein. Later in the season there are the sugar rich berries of arctic shrubs to feed on. Secondly, the continuous daylight hours mean that the birds can remain active for longer with only the minimum of time set aside for resting and

Studies of adult and young barnacle geese. In a good breeding season an adult pair will successfully raise 3 or even 4 young. But in poor years when the summer weather is severe they will fail to produce any young at all.

MOULT MIGRATION

A party of pink-footed geese in Deltadal. Moult migration happens in species that shed their flight feathers simultaneously rendering them flightless and vulnerable for a few short weeks each year. It is a strategy highly developed in geese.

Among a population on the breeding grounds are numerous immature and non-breeding and failed breeding birds, which if they all stayed within the same general area, would be in direct competition for the available resources with nesting birds trying to raise young. In moult migration they withdraw at this critical stage to sites that are safe, secluded and with plentiful food where they can moult.

Many thousands of pink-footed geese from Iceland are involved in a moult migration to north-east Greenland. The advantages of going such a long distance is that they not only avoid competition, but in higher latitudes plant growth is at an earlier stage and therefore more nutritious than if the moult migration had taken them south of the breeding range where the food available would be past its peak. The main disadvantage is that further north the arctic climate is more unpredictable, and when it is time to head south the return journey is longer.

---

bathing. Lastly, geese are one of only a very few herbivores in the arctic and the only ones to feed their young entirely on plant food. Direct competition for the resource is avoided as the other main arctic herbivores like muskox and reindeer are thinly spread and frequently absent altogether from large areas. But there are disadvantages and certain dangers for birds that breed in the high Arctic. Undertaking long migrations involves storing sufficient energy reserves to fuel the flight. The use of staging areas allows these reserves to be replenished, enough for some species to be up to 20% above their normal weight on arrival. This strategy is an insurance against the climate.

For most large breeding birds the period of summer which is completely snow-free is just too short; here in Scoresby Land the snow melts in June, but by the end of August or early September there are heavy frosts and it is already starting to snow again. There is not enough time to establish a nest site, lay eggs, incubate, hatch the egg and raise the young to the flying stage, so the birds must start the breeding cycle before the onset of the main thaw. This means that early in the season their supply of food is inaccessible under the snow. For the first few weeks of the breeding season they are dependent on their reserves of energy. In years when the spring weather is particularly harsh and the start of the breeding season seriously delayed, there is the danger of being caught by the first snows of winter. If the spring is particularly severe, attempts at breeding may be abandoned altogether. However, most populations of geese breeding in the Arctic are able to withstand periodic breeding failures, for in good summers they almost always have a high breeding-success rate.

I have been watching the flock of feeding barnacle geese for 15 minutes or more and they have moved closer in towards the hill – but are still a long way off. I need to change my sketch-pads, so carefully I start to move. Instantly a ripple of barking alarm calls shoots through the flock and clustering together they race off across the tundra. It is obvious that they would be very wary, but I had not reckoned on them being quite so nervous. If I had been an Arctic fox I would have certainly missed a meal.

From the col of Hestepas high above Mesters Vig the view is stunning; far away on the other side of King Oscars Fjord the mountain ridges and pinnacles of Traill Island, bathed in warm morning sunshine, rise above a band of cold sea-mist running up the fjord from the open sea like a strip of silvery paper pasted along the horizon. Fingers of mist creeping in the light breeze up the coast turn away from the mouth of Mesters Vig below me. With virtually no wind and a cloudless sky of deep icy blue, a classic arctic summer's day is in the making.

A pair of ringed plovers, that are breeding in the boulder fan at the top of the col, protest my lingering presence so I begin the long climb down into Mesters Vig and along the shore towards Deltadal; carrying my 'studio' on my back, as well as food, tent and sleeping bag, it will take me half a day. The gravel slopes and spongy terraces on the way down are thick with flowers – arnica and harebell, the bright yellow of hawkweed, white bell heather and mountain avens. A sprinkling of Arctic redpolls lift off a patch of blueberry and a ptarmigan with chicks crouch low as I approach, but sit tight as I pass. A glaucous gull drifts by overhead, circles once then flies on its way up the valley. For a while I follow the tracks of an Arctic fox weaving along the shore between blocks of stranded ice and lines of flotsam made up almost entirely of shed goose feathers; most are from pink-feet. Here and there on gravel spits and short grassy areas close to the shore are places where they must have rested for a while and preened as there is a thicker layer of feathers and masses of droppings.

A juvenile arctica *dunlin feeding among mossy pools at Mesters Vig in early August. It is now on its own, and while the food remains plentiful and the arctic summer still holds, it will feed busily storing energy for the forthcoming journey. Soon it will join up with other dunlin on the coast and then, in three or four weeks time, the flock will set off for Iceland, their first staging post on the journey to Africa.*

I have learned quickly to look up when a raven, or an Arctic or long-tailed skua calls. This time an Arctic fox is being mobbed as it passes through the territory of a pair of long-tailed skuas. With a flight as light as a tern but as powerful as a falcon they swoop and dive at the fox, calling noisily. The fox, head down, turns to snap as they make each pass. I watch the skuas long after the fox has gone and I see their chick moving between the boulders. It is about half-fledged as there is still a lot of down on the head and body, but the cold browns of the juvenile plumage are showing well. The skuas will soon leave here and head out far into the Atlantic Ocean for the winter, to return again next May or early June.

Some way offshore a flock of 30 or 40 pink-footed geese, accompanying numerous youngsters, swim slowly through the maze of drifting ice, they would have seen me coming and raced for the safety of water long before I saw them.

It is late afternoon and I have at last reached the massive boulder fans and undulating gravel moraines that slope away from the steep valley sides down towards the enormous web of braided channels of Deltadal. Ahead of me is an undulating tundra landscape of boggy hollows, river channels, dry heaths and moss banks that fills the head of the valley.

The breeding waders of the arctic are the birds that I want to get to grips with now and the south facing habitats of Deltadal are just the place to be for that. South facing slopes are extremely important ecologically in the Arctic. Tilted towards the sun they catch more warmth and are among the first areas to become snow-free in spring, crucial to birds that must begin the breeding season early. Wet areas on the slopes are vital in the life cycles of many arthropods that have aquatic stages, particularly the non-biting midges which are by far the most abundant of arctic insects. The ecology of the arctic tundra in summer also includes a host of saw flies, crane flies, mayflies, mosquitoes and other insect species, most of which live their lives close to the ground in the warmest layer of air. This seasonal abundance of insect food, readily available in the mass of wet and watery habitats, is vitally important to waders.

Seeing a lone sanderling feeding between the moss banks and pools I settle down to watch and paint. From its bright spangled juvenile plumage it is easy to tell that it is one of this year's birds.

In a while two more sanderling appear and begin feeding, but these two are adults. After the rigours of the breeding season their feathers are well worn and lying less neatly than the juvenile plumage and, after months of exposure to sunlight, the colours look more bleached.

As the day wears on, strands of high cloud begin to build inland over the mountains and within an hour the veil has covered the sun and it turns colder. A small herd of muskox move onto the slopes below Hjørnet and on the heathy gravel mounds ahead a ringed plover starts calling. Then, much closer in, I catch a movement in the corner of my eye. Gently tilting the telescope I focus the lens on an adult knot that is feeding leisurely among the boulders and mossy hummocks at the edge of a stream; but more than that, it is accompanied by two almost fully fledged chicks that still have a few wisps of down left clinging to the tips of the scapulars and tail feathers.

At the northern limits of my travels on migration, I could not have wished for better views of a species more appropriate to my story. Knot are superlative waders, travelling great distances at incredible speeds and I have got to know them well during the journey. Here in Deltadal, at a fraction over 72°N, they are at the southern edge of their breeding range in this part of Greenland. I am doubly lucky because they are thinly spread hereabouts.

The adult is in worn summer plumage and in this state the sexes are virtually indistinguishable, but I suspect this is a male bird. Like the spotted redshank in the Scandinavian taiga, the female knot, having laid the eggs and tended the small young, leave the males to look after the growing young until they fledge. The southbound females, often in company with various failed, non-breeding, or immature birds make up the first wave of early migrants. The next wave will be mostly made up of male birds leaving the juveniles to linger on the breeding grounds until they head south. Waves like these are characteristic of the autumn migration of waders.

The three knot continue feeding, picking and probing continuously while staying quite close; working forward in the same general direction they gradually move out of the pool system, cross a wide fan of boulders and continue across the slopes and eventually out of sight.

An adult (left) and a juvenile knot at Mesters Vig. The distinctively plumaged juvenile will partially moult sometime between early September and Decmber. In this first non-breeding plumage it will superficially resemble the adult; the subtle differences are only detectable when a bird is in the hand.

The clear bright skies of the past few days have given way now to a low ceiling of cloud that hangs above the mountain walls and clings to their icy peaks. It is the 8th of August and already there is more than a hint of winter in the weather. A dusting of snow fell last night and the wind has turned much colder. Yesterday I walked back round from Deltadal to this area of sweeping outwash fans, undulating gravel plains and level heaths on the coast between Nyhavn and Skeldal. Thick carpets of mosses and lichens hug every contour, brightened here and there with patches of deep violet broad-leafed willow herb and yellow mountain saxifrage. Boggy pools thick with cotton grass and sedgy fens fill the hollows. There is a pair of red-throated divers breeding on one of the ponds. When I left for Deltadal a week ago it looked as if they were still incubating as one of the adults hugged the nest closely when I appeared, but this morning both adults are out on the open water and between them bobs the dark sooty-brown chick. In about six or seven weeks time, when the chick is strong enough to fly, they will move down to the sea together and linger there until the sea-ice begins to form at the end of September. Then they will leave these arctic waters and migrate southwards to winter at sea somewhere close to the coastline of western Europe.

Alerted by a raven calling I look up to see a gyrfalcon, the most majestic bird of arctic regions. It is moving fast and twisting and turning to shake off both the raven and an Arctic skua that has joined in the mobbing.

A small flock of turnstones passing down the coast as a bank of sea-mist rolls in.

From a distance I watch a party of wheatears on the lower slopes of the Nyhavn hills, and because it has perhaps the most remarkable migration of any small land-bird, I move my 'studio' across there to take a much closer look at them.

There are three races of the Eurasian wheatear *Oenanthe oenanthe*. The summer breeding range of the nominate *oenanthe* race is from the Atlantic coast of Europe across northern Asia as far as the eastern extremes of Siberia, with small numbers then crossing the Bering Sea to breed in Alaska. The further north you go the larger the races become. The *schileri* form which breeds in Iceland, the Faeroes and Jan Mayen Island, is intermediate between *oenanthe* and the third form *leucorhoa*, or the Greenland wheatear, which breeds in Greenland and the fringes of northeastern Canada. As well as being larger than the nominate race, the Greenland wheatear is more richly coloured on the throat and chest.

OPPOSITE
A juvenile Greenland wheatear, a slightly larger and more richly coloured race of the nominate 'northern' wheatear. In a few days time this young bird will face a journey of 8000 km to Africa.

From down the slopes towards the beach comes the irregular musical rattle of a flock of turnstones on the move. They circle above the hillside for a minute or two then land together on the dry heathy slopes and begin feeding. In a while a large flock of sanderling sweep above the valley calling all the time, then tumble quickly down into a wide gulley to feed on the 'meadows' of moss and cotton grass bogs. Earlier, over the other side of the hills, there were small flocks of dunlin on the move. This wader activity is a sure sign that the arctic summer will soon be over. Already some birds will have left, but these flocks are gathering in preparation for the journey ahead and will leave in waves over the coming few days and weeks.

The wheatears too will soon be leaving and, like the waders, are now busy feeding to lay down sufficient reserves of fat for the long journey ahead. In two or three weeks time, towards the end of August, the exodus will be well underway. After making landfall in Europe, they will turn south-west, passing down through southern Europe and north Africa to reach their sub-Saharan winter quarters in West Africa, from Sénégal and Sierra Leone eastwards into Mali.

Having finished work on the wheatears I depot my equipment and walk up into the Nyhavn hills. In the very late evening, as the wind strengthens, it turns much colder, but the cloud begins to lift. An hour or more before midnight the sun drops below the far peaks at the head of Kong Oscars Fjord, already it is sinking fast towards the 'dark time' of winter. In two weeks time the first frosts will come during the few hours of darkness, and by the last week of September the fjord will be frozen over. In mid-November the sun will finally disappear below the skylines of Mesters Vig, but by then the migrants that travelled here for the short arctic summer will be far away in their winter homes.

CHAPTER FOUR

From Cloud to Cloud

And fainter onward, like wild birds that change
Their seasons in the night, and wail their way
From cloud to cloud, down the long wind the dream
Shrill'd; but in going mingled with dim cries
Far in the moonlit haze among the hills
Tennyson, *The Passing of Arthur*

It is still early August, but much has changed since I last checked my local patch near the village. The day has been hot and hazy but now in late afternoon it is beginning to turn thundery. Huge columns of smoke rising from stubble fires curdle with the cloud. Swifts are milling about against the sultry greys and smoky browns in the sky. Soon the they will be gone as they are among the first birds to leave in the autumn.

The lanes are no longer filled with full summer song, but there are still plenty of birds about. A whitethroat chatters hesitatingly from the thick cover of a hedge. Swallows sweep back and forth across the fields and bunches of chattering house martins cluster around the farm buildings. On the tyre tracks in the lane a spotted flycatcher tussles with a peacock butterfly, stabbing and flipping it in the way a song thrush deals with a snail. It takes a while for the victim to be subdued. Then the bird flies off with the butterfly in its bill to feed young nearby, possibly a second brood.

Turning through the gate into the sloping meadow a startled juvenile cuckoo clatters from a hawthorn, its rich barred plumage showing clearly. After fledging sometime in July young cuckoos wander for a while in their natal neighbourhood before setting out alone on the long journey to Africa. Adult birds set off on migration in August, before the juveniles; few cuckoos of any age are left in Britain or Europe beyond the beginning of September.

I turn down the grassy track that leads towards the 'hobby oak' set up my telescope and sit down to wait. In time the unmistakable silhouette of a hobby drifts out from the wood. As it circles and tilts against the evening light the dark brownish upperparts and more thickly streaked underparts of a juvenile show clearly. It is getting late when one of the adults appears. Last year two young were raised here and I would have thought that after the fine summer they should have had an equally successful breeding season. By the time I leave, still with only one sighting of one young bird, I cannot quantify their breeding success this year. By late August or early September

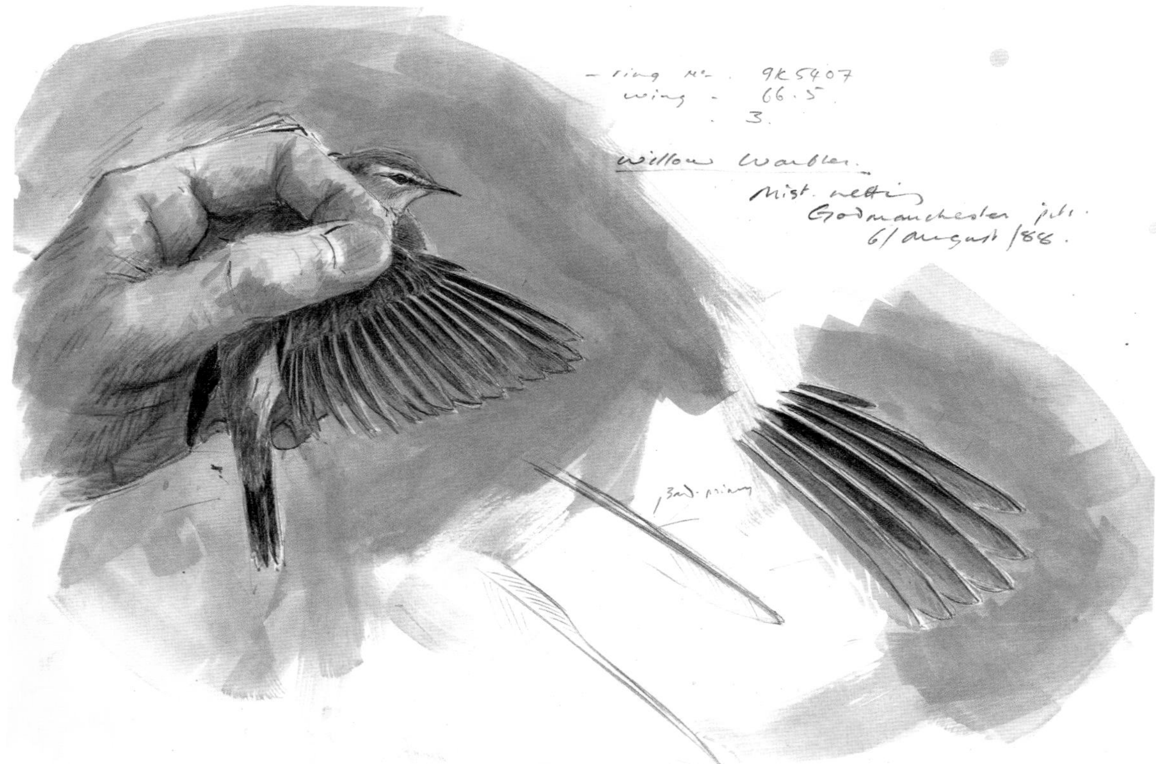

A willow warbler with wing held to show shape and lengths of primary feathers.

OPPOSITE
Swallows assembling in autumn before their journey south. Little Gransden, Cambridgeshire.

the southward passage of hobbies will begin and by mid-October very few birds will be left in temperate latitudes.

The hobby is one of the most aerobatic of falcons. Slim-lined and long-winged they can manoeuvre with superb agility and are capable of strong sustained flight. They use their aerial agility to catch and often feed on small birds and insects on the wing. With such flying abilities and 'in flight' feeding skills a bird like a hobby seems superbly adapted to make a long migratory journey. Migration could be seen merely as an extension of its normal daily life.

However, large numbers of migrants have a style of flight, which although best suited to their method of feeding, appears to conflict with their need to migrate. Small warblers for example, that forage among leaves for insects, need short rounded wings to flutter efficiently in the tree canopy, but to fly great distances they would ideally require a longer and narrower wing shape. The way in which many migrants resolve these conflicting needs is strikingly revealed in wing shapes, particularly evident in closely related species that are either migratory or sedentary; Cetti's and sedge warblers for example.

Cetti's warbler is a shy skulking bird of dense shrubby waterside vegetation. The form that is found in the western Palearctic range, where it is resident for the whole year, has a wing that is relatively short and broad. The sedge warbler on the other hand is a highly migratory species accomplishing the journey to Africa with very long flights between a few staging areas; its wing shape is much more sharply profiled. Similar differences,

A juvenile sedge warbler after ringing. For much of the year a sedge warbler weighs between about 10gms or 12gms but before migration it almost doubles its weight.

though less marked, can be seen in the closely related willow warbler and chiffchaff, both of them migrants but each travelling relatively shorter and longer distances respectively.

The migratory tendency in birds has also modified feeding strategies, particularly during the build-up period before the journey. Most migrations are not triggered by immediate hunger, but begin at a time of food abundance when the birds can lay down reserves of energy. They have also evolved flying strategies to make efficient use of the 'fuel' they store: they fly at certain heights, at night, or at optimum speeds.

The changes in a migrant's physiology that enable it to make the journey, must also be integrated with the moult. For a species to survive, successful breeding is obviously of the greatest importance and migration increases the annual survival chances for a particular species. But for an individual bird to survive, feather maintenance and renewal or moult is crucially important. It is one of the most important aspects of a bird's annual life cycle.

In the course of a year, individual feathers suffer from wear and tear. They are damaged and abraded by sticks and branches, sunlight, and feather-lice. In time the plumage begins to lose its strength. Before all these effects threaten the bird's survival, by bad insulation or inability to fly, the plumage must be replaced. But moult has its own disadvantages; it places additional energy demands on the bird as extra protein is needed to grow the new feather. As the old feather falls and before the new one is grown, the efficiency of the bird's insulation will be reduced and more energy will be needed to maintain body temperature. Missing flight feathers during

Wing shapes of (from top to bottom) willow warbler, sedge warbler, chiffchaff and Cetti's warbler.

moult will make flying less efficient, requiring more energy to stay airborne. Because of its extra physiological demands, the pattern and timing of moult in the annual cycle of the bird's life is crucial and varies between species. The advantages and disadvantages must be balanced and the process fitted in between breeding and migration, or when there is sufficient food available to generate the extra energy required. Generally, the strategy adopted by a migrant species is related to the location of its breeding and wintering areas, and the way in which it makes the journey between them. The moult could be undertaken during the breeding cycle while still attending young, or it could be accomplished rapidly between the end of breeding and before migration. Alternatively a species could begin the moult on the breeding grounds and then suspend the process, resuming or completing it either in favourable locations en route, or later on in the winter quarters. Another strategy could be to migrate and then undergo a complete moult in the wintering area.

Whatever the strategy, moult in birds falls into two broad categories; a complete moult, usually undertaken once a year; and a partial moult, when only some of the feathers are replaced, sometimes more than once a year. In both, feather replacement is not random but follows a basic sequential pattern which is very similar in most birds. The patterns can be scored most easily in the main flight feathers and in the tail, but a bird must be in the hand to score moult correctly.

The Wash Wader Ringing Group are experts at getting birds in the hand. Since they started about 30 years ago, about 175,000 birds have been caught and studied by them at various sites on the saltings and fields surrounding the Wash, a vast and shallow expanse of silt and saltmarsh, tidal creeks and sandbanks trapped between the coasts of Norfolk and Lincolnshire. It is the most important site for birds on the east coast of Britain, particularly during the spring and autumn migration when over 200,000 wintering waders and wildfowl are joined by over a quarter of a million passage birds. Dunlin arriving for the winter from northern Europe and the USSR pass others from Greenland en route to Morocco; bar-tailed godwits from northern Russia pausing on their way to Sénégal; knot from the Canadian arctic feed alongside others from Siberia en route to Mauritania. Every night during the migration season countless small migrants like warblers, flycatchers, chats and pipits, pass overhead on their way down to southern Europe, or north and sub-Saharan Africa. Each species making the journey will have its own moult strategy adapted to its pattern of migration, and those patterns and strategies are best seen close up by looking at birds in the hand.

At first light on August 10th I am wedged in a hide between three members of the ringing group and a tangle of command wires, spades, sacking and electrical junction boxes. There are still two hours until high tide.

A skim of mist lying across the fields has spilled over the sea-wall and out to the saltings where in the grey half-light there is a constant flow of birds across the flatness of the Wash – flocks of turnstone, dunlin, curlew, grey

plovers, whimbrel and bar-tailed godwits all on the move with the speed of the incoming tide.

Through a slit in the sacking I watch a little tern fishing the borrow dyke in front of the hide and a passing yellow wagtail pauses for a while on the hide roof, calls once or twice then moves on. There are wheatears on the sea-wall and the saltings where they are joined by a flock of starlings that are feeding in a tight bunch close to the hidden nets.

With the suddenness of a tap turning on the tide reaches the lip of the borrow dyke and starts pouring in. Radio contact is more frequent and hurried now.

'Have you got any grey plover your end'?

'There are some redshank up and coming your way. Try and watch where they go'.

'The starlings have been spooked.' I look through the slit as a roar erupts from further down the saltings, 'some of the birds are up with them'. Luckily, when the tide peaks the mass of birds have settled again – right where we want them, close to the nets.

A little stint, centre left, and a dunlin part way through its moult, top right, on the Wash in late September.

A bar-tailed godwit and juvenile curlew sandpiper.

Thud! The cannons fire.

Activity for the next twenty minutes or half-hour is intense, but by the time processing of the catch begins the now familiar relaxed precision of bird ringers at work has already descended on the temporary encampment spread out in the open air. Today's catch is mostly dunlin and there are a few turnstones as well, but the biggest surprise is a whimbrel – they catch very few on the Wash. In thirty years they have caught well over 90,000 dunlin and 5000 turnstone, but less than 100 whimbrel.

Many hours of patient systematic studies like this have enabled the movements and moult strategies of some waders to be worked out in detail.

Ringing studies of 1500 grey plovers by the group have found that their moulting behaviour is different from that of any other wader that occurs there. Of those birds arriving in early autumn about 40% are in arrested primary moult. Most resume their moult at the Wash, completing the process by November. But a significant proportion do not leaving one, two or sometimes three outer primaries unmoulted until the following March when they are replaced. It seems that there are advantages to moulting some innermost primaries before leaving the high arctic breeding grounds; there is less to be done after arriving at the main moulting and wintering areas like the Wash where they must put on a lot of weight by November in readiness

for the hardships of winter. So those birds that have not completed their primary moult by then find it advantageous to arrest moult and channel their energies instead into depositing fat reserves rather than growing large wing feathers. When better weather and good feeding conditions come in spring, wing moult can be resumed in readiness for the northward migration.

Very few whimbrel winter in western Europe, with only a handful remaining behind in Portugal and southern Spain. This individual, along with the other autumn birds, will be from breeding grounds in Scandinavia or north-west Russia on passage to the main wintering grounds on the coastal fringes of tropical Africa.

For the past two days south-westerly winds have brought wet and blustery weather, but this morning, September 7th, the wind has turned more northerly and is a lot colder. For over two hours, against an early autumn sky that is clear and bright, I have been watching the space and favoured perches around the 'Hobby Oak', but have seen nothing yet. It looks as if sometime in the past three days, since I was here last, the hobbies have set off on their long journey to Africa. I wish I had seen them leave.

September 11th and it is one of those days that carries more than a hint of autumn. Looking out over the fens of Cambridgeshire from the high bank by Welch's Dam on the Ouse or Hundred Foot Washes, on one side are

The Ouse Washes in early autumn, with juvenile ruff, snipe, lapwing and passing sand martins.

the damp meadows of the RSPB and Bedfordshire and Cambridgeshire Wildlife Trust reserves, and stretching away on the other is the peaty brown flatness of fenland fields. The day is warm with a wind from the south-west which is tugging tightly bunched stacks of cloud and their shadows across the flatness of the landscape. On the wind are the busy autumnal agricultural sounds of grain dryers, tractors and harvesters in the distance, and there is the smell of burnt stubble in the air. A kestrel sweeps low down the sheltered side of the bank and slips quickly over the top of the dam, causing the lines of swallows, and house and sand martins on the cables strung across the river to fall away in a chattering shower.

Crossing the bridge at the dam, I walk down towards the viewing hides on the RSPB reserve, through the flocks of sheep grazing the rough grass behind the high river bank. Showers of yellow wagtails rise out of the grazing sheep, circle round and settle back down behind me as I pass. Some of these birds will be passing through on their way south; others will have spent the summer here on the washes. Many are juveniles, distinctive in their duskier plumage that lacks the brighter colours of the adults. At this end of the year the adults will be just about through their complete annual moult after the breeding season, and although brighter than the young birds, they now lack the sparkling yellows and olive greens of the birds that I saw arriving here in fresh breeding plumage almost four months ago. There are still good numbers of yellow wagtails about – but not for long. Their autumn migration is already well underway and each night a few more flocks depart. In two or three weeks time they will all have gone.

The heavy rain last week has left plenty of shallow pools and soft mud,

conditions that are particularly good for waders, and there are good numbers about today. At the edge of the farthest pool are four greenshanks and behind them on the mud a small party of curlew sandpipers. In a more sheltered shallow, a lone green sandpiper wades belly deep picking at the water surface as it goes. Most of these passage birds will end their journey in the main wintering areas of the Mediterranean basin and Africa south of the Sahara leaving behind somewhere between 500 and 1000 individuals in southern Britain and Ireland where they are at the northern limit of their wintering range. It is late for this particular green sandpiper to be passing through, so it is possible that it will be one of the very few that will stay for the whole winter, so long as the weather does not deteriorate. If it does it will be forced to move south or perhaps leave the British Isles altogether to escape the freeze that will have locked up its food.

A green sandpiper (main picture), snipe and ruff. Green sandpipers are particularly early return migrants being regularly recorded in mid-June with the peak passage occurring in August.

Closer to the hide, on a larger expanse of water and mud, are ten or twelve snipe and mixed in with them are a handful of ruff. Many of the migrant ruff arriving in autumn in Britain are breeding birds from Scandinavia and the USSR, on passage to wintering areas further south. One ruff, ringed during its winter stay in Britain, was found the following breeding season near Yakutsk in the far reaches of Siberia, a distance of 7500 kilometres.

In the softer light of early evening I walk on to a hide further down the washes again passing through the sheep and yellow wagtails, and this time through a charm of goldfinches working their way from thistle to thistle down the river bank. Numerous swallows are slipping and sliding easily into the wind, sometimes dropping low over the river to skim a sip of water

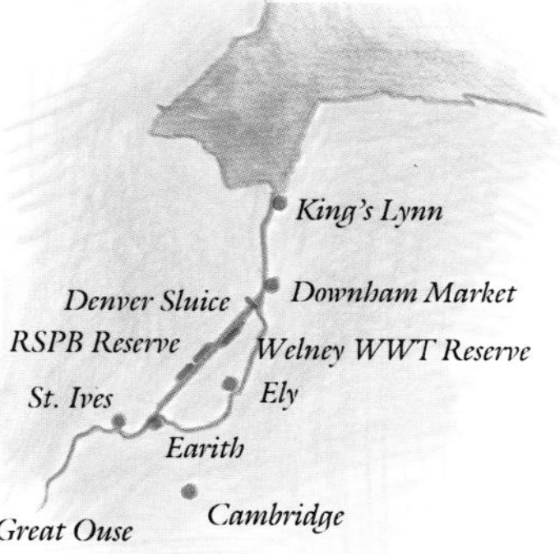

from the surface. I turn quickly when I hear a mixed bunch of sand martins and swallows suddenly start chattering, just in time to see a hobby dashing pass them without striking.

Ahead, two birdwatchers are walking up from the hide I am heading for, and slowing down as we draw level one of them asks, "Had much today?"

"Yes – not bad" I reply. "I've just had a hobby and there's a good mix of waders from the next hide. The usual for this time of year; you know...curlew sands and one green sand...a few ruff...but nothing special. How about you?"

"We had a spotted crake this afternoon from there" says one of them quite excitedly, turning to point at the next hide along the washes. "but I do not know whether it's still there", he adds cautiously.

"We had good views of it", says the other fellow.

"Thanks, I'll try my luck from there then...Cheers".

"Good luck".

My trouble is that when I am out painting I sometimes settle for hours in one spot. Often it is a hide, but usually I set my stool in the corner of a landscape where I can sit quietly with sketchbooks and telescope and lose myself in the field of view, the light, and of course the action of the birds. The elements of wildlife, light and landscape are all inseparable parts of the same picture; to get one without the other would leave on paper only fragments of a much more important whole.

Charging about clutching brushes, paper, paints and easel, in the hope of snatching something here or a bird there, is fraught with difficulty. Each time I would have to pack the paints away, water would be spilled and colours smudged. Better to sit quietly in one spot. If I sit there long enough, it is likely that most of 'what's about' will pass by and I can put it down on paper. That is the theory, but by working this way I sometimes miss out on 'good birds' that unbeknown to me are creating great interest a short distance away from where I am sitting. Today could turn out to be one of those days. For an artist on migration, spotted crake would be a good bird to get down on paper.

The spotted crake is one of the most unlikely of migrants. With its compact and oval shape, and gangly legs and stubby tail, it would seem to be almost incapable of flight. They are secretive skulking birds seldom venturing far from wet and tangled vegetation. Surprisingly, however, like the most of the crakes and rails in the western Palearctic, the spotted crake is capable of long-distance migration with the largest numbers crossing the Sahara to winter in Africa.

With only about an hour of daylight left, I settle in the second hide and look out across the washes again. On the far side of one of the pools are a few snipe and a lone ruff, another male. Black-headed gulls, coots, mallards and teal are spread out on the water. High in a willow tree a lone turtle dove rests for a while. A flock of dunlin rush down the wind, turn suddenly in a compact bunch, rise and fall for a moment, then land together.

On the far side of one of the pools a lapwing calls and flies up into the wind pulling a string of others with it. As the last lapwing rises, a single wood sandpiper flashes up as well. This bird is on passage and still has a

A yellow-browed warbler in the pines at Holkham on the North Norfolk coast. They are small Phylloscopus *or 'leaf warblers' that are one of the most regular vagrants to wander west into Europe at migration times. There are usually less than 100 recorded in Britain and Ireland each year, but in some years there are unusually large numbers.*

long way to go if it is heading for tropical Africa where the majority of wood sandpipers spend the winter. Not long from now it will be on its way south again at impressive speed. One wood sandpiper ringed in Sweden, was found the next day 1075km further south in Italy. Somewhere in southern Europe it will stop once more and, after feeding for a while, will fly non-stop across the Mediterranean and Sahara desert to tropical Africa.

As the light softens and the shadows lengthen, a flight of teal come in past a line of cormorants flying to roost up the washes. A hidden moorhen trills once from the ditch below the hide. I stop drawing and through the telescope carefully scan the water margins once more. A blackbird begins its distinctive and persistent call *pink.. pink...... pink...... pink.....pink..pink*. And suddenly there it is! The spotted crake! It must have been feeding out of sight for some time behind the thick vegetation, as it now skulks into view slowly edging around a muddy corner. The moment of full view is brief as it is soon picking its way round the back edge of the vegetation again, with only glimpses of movement behind the stems; until it crosses an open area of mud, then the views are longer. It is a fabulous bird.

The air space in which birds move is characteristically unstable, filled with every kind of weather system, from complex and constantly changing patterns of anticyclonic 'highs' that are relatively stable systems that often linger for several days having little or no wind and usually clear skies, to cyclonic 'lows', which produce a vigorous turmoil of strong winds, heavy cloud and belts of rain. Weather systems can either be short lived and effect a small area, or persist and cover a very wide area. Whatever their degree, they inevitably affect the inception, progress, performance and duration of a migrant bird in flight.

It is probable that a small bird, already physiologically primed for the migratory flight, assesses the current local weather situation and when it finds an anticyclonic pattern of clear skies to aid navigation, and favourable winds to speed it on its way, it departs. If these optimum conditions persist the migrant is able to fly with little risk of drifting away from the heading it is trying to maintain. But dense low cloud or fog, heavy rain, or strong winds can delay the start of migration or halt progress altogether. Severe conditions also hinder navigation by obscuring the clues they need to find their way. A bird cannot reliably predict the best migrating conditions, but so long as food remains plentiful a migrant can afford to delay departure until conditions for travelling become favourable. However, the longer the start is delayed, the more readily will a migrant depart even if conditions are less than favourable. There is a limit to how long a bird can 'hold on'. Once the journey has begun, wind speed and direction are the most important factors affecting migration.

Drifting will depend largely on the size, weight and flying power of the bird, but they can compensate for the effects of migrational drift and re-orientate themselves, with the degree of ability to correct varying between individuals and species. Experienced adults, better able to judge conditions at departure, are less prone to displacement and more able to re-orientate when they are off course. When birds are grounded, the largest numbers are usually found to be immature birds. In early September 1965, in one of the most remarkable and massive falls ever seen in the British Isles, it was estimated that half a million birds came to ground along 40 kilometres of Suffolk coastline – redstarts, whitethroats, wheatears, pied flycatchers, garden and willow warblers. Within days as the wind veered and the cloud broke up, the majority of birds were able to move on.

Disorientated birds drifting off course in poor conditions are reliant on their fixed fat reserves to keep them going, and as the supply begins to dwindle they must seek a place to rest before total exhaustion engulfs them. For a small bird that has drifted far out to sea the only refuge might be a passing ship or an oil drilling platform and accounts of birds collapsing exhausted on decks are many. But for every one that finds a refuge for a while, there will be many others that perish in the sea.

Another way in which we sometimes catch a glimpse of the usually unseen movements of migrants, and witness how climatic events can overtake them, is due to lighthouses. Positioned as they are on coastal promontories with powerful beams visible in almost every extreme of foul weather, they can interrupt the passage of birds sometimes with disastrous results.

When the peak migration season coincides with a sudden deterioration in the weather and a mass exodus of birds, those already underway will quickly

The lighthouse and shingle banks at Dungeness on the tip of southern Britain on the last day of September. A fine autumn day with a good passage of birds.

become disorientated at night if the only point of reference in heavily overcast or foggy conditions is the brilliant flash of a revolving light. Then they crowd into the beams. Some come to ground, others struggle past, but others spiral into the light, eventually crashing into the lantern glass. On bad nights hundreds of birds can be killed – redwings, starlings, water rails, grasshopper and sedge warblers; whatever is passing within range.

I remember an October night 15 years ago at the lighthouse on Bardsey Island, off the Lleyn Peninsula in north Wales. It was blowing hard and raining as I stood in the lantern room, the mechanical rattle of the revolving lens behind me almost drowned by the fierce rush of wind and rain lashing the tower outside. A confusion of fluttering redwings and starlings were frozen in the beam every few seconds – then came the crack of bone or scratch of claw or beak against the glass. For a moment a short-eared owl appeared in the lights then drifted back into the darkness. Just before dawn there were only a few birds still around the tower, but lying on the ground beneath lay 30 or 40 dead ones.

Heinrich Gätke on Helgoland in the early 1900s watched a lighthouse attraction and wrote:

> *The whole sky is now filled with a babble of hundreds of thousands of voices, and as we approach the lighthouse there presents itself to the eye the scene which more than confirms the experience of the ear. Under the intense glare of the light swarms of larks, starlings and thrushes career around in ever varying density like showers of brilliant sparks or huge snowflakes driven onward by a gale and continuously replaced as they disappear by freshly arriving multitudes.*

The enormous geographical scale of migration implied in a 'fall' or an 'attraction', and the huge numbers of birds sometimes involved, is dramatic, but what they really do is give a sense of scale to our perception of migration. They let us glimpse a fraction of the countless millions of migrants that night after night usually pass overhead unseen in the darkness as they move with the seasons.

CHAPTER FIVE

Down the Long Wind

The Atlantic coast of France has some of the most important wetlands for migratory birds in western Europe. From Brittany to Biarritz there are huge inter-tidal inlets, estuaries, marshes and lagoons, all of them sites that are vital as staging areas for passage birds, or as wintering sites for large numbers of wildfowl and waders. But unfortunately not many of them offer safety or peace. In France birdwatchers are greatly outnumbered by hunters. Despite legislation to protect most bird species, French hunters not only shoot over two million wildfowl each year, but also about a million turtle doves, about 25 million thrushes and goodness knows how many raptors, as well as a host of other species. Yesterday I sat with Denis Bredin of the *Ligue Française pour la Protection des Oiseaux* (LPO) in their offices on the waterfront at Rochefort on the Biscay coast. He told me of many migrant waders like black-tailed godwits, curlew and redshank that also fall victim each year to hunters' guns.

In 1986 the LPO established a small reserve in a corner of the huge bay trapped between the Ile d'Oléron and the stretch of coastline from Rochefort to La Rochelle. The reserve is an area of meadow and marshland behind the sea-wall, but also includes a segment of inter-tidal mudflats and saltings beyond the wall. Wintering birds were quick to change their habits

and make use of the reserve; in its first two winters the numbers seeking safe refuge there doubled.

Last night, after leaving Denis, I parked the van in a quiet sheltered spot between the reserve and the tiny village of Brouage. Before turning in I noted the skies were clear and there was a gentle north-easterly breeze blowing – a good night for migrants to travel.

Sometime in the night the wind died, leaving a thin film of mist lying over the meadows as I set out at dawn. In the soft grey half-light I watch from the sea-wall as three hen harriers rise from their roost in a patch of rough ground. There are snipe about and a green sandpiper that lifts suddenly out of a darkened ditch as I make my way around the edge of the saltings. The sound of distant gunfire rolls across the mudflats in the stillness of early morning.

High tide is at twenty past six, so there are plenty of waders on the move; a string of 15 or 20 avocets with a few black-winged stilts trailing behind and flocks of dunlin and bar-tailed godwits, curlew and oystercatchers, ringed and Kentish plovers. I can hear skylarks passing and a party of yellow wagtails moving down the tideline. A line of junipers spaced along a bank of stranded shells is full of chiffchaffs, robins and redstarts, and on the sweep of shells are wheatears and a short-toed lark as well.

The sudden movement of a camouflaged hunter under the sea-wall startles me. He is sitting in the shadow of the sign post marking the edge of the reserve, so he could not be any closer without actually entering the sanctuary.

Further down the saltings I sit sketching until late morning, accompanied by the sound of the tide and every few minutes the noise of gunfire, some of it from distant fields and some from the mudflats and saltings. Perhaps

A wheatear in the early morning on the coast of France.

each time it is a different victim; a whimbrel, or maybe a spotted redshank, a grey plover, coot or mallard.

High tide this evening on the eastern side of the Ile d'Oléron is at half past seven and Denis had suggested a couple of good locations. In the heat of afternoon I weave slowly through the island's fabulous landscape of low sandy hills and pine woods, past old farmhouses and barns and red-tiled white-walled houses, around a lattice of lagoons and oysterbeds, reed-filled ditches and here and there fields of sunflowers sprinkled with goldfinches and linnets. It is a landscape that has great grey shrike, marsh harrier, Cetti's warbler, bluethroat, and an osprey. It is a young bird, this year's brood, on migration for the first time. As it fishes one of the lagoons, its pale and variegated upperparts show clearly in the bright sunlight.

At the Pointe d'Arceau there are stands of cypress and locust trees with lines of juniper running along the shore. By late afternoon I have set up my 'studio' just beyond them on a strand line of shells and tidal junk where bright green and speckled black wall lizards scurry.

For the next hour or more, as the tide creeps higher, the waders feed and shift about the saltings, sand-bars and mud until the evening light begins to glow. Then, as strings of little egrets start heading inland to roost a skein of brent geese – about 20 or 25 birds in all – fly down the coast. I had certainly not expected to see them here. These are dark-bellied birds that will only just have arrived from their Siberian breeding grounds.

The image of geese and egrets together reinforces a sense of overlap and transition of seasons and birds. The egrets, about ready to leave for their winter quarters in sub-Saharan Africa, are at the northern limit of their warm-temperate and tropical breeding range; the geese, beginning their winter sojourn, are at the southern limits of their winter range. Around about here at migration times it seems to me that a little bit of the arctic meets the tropics. But hunting pressures make this part of France a dangerous place for birds; yet further south in France, and in many other countries around the Mediterranean, the seasonal slaughter of birds is even more horrifying.

Even before the sun climbed above the mountainous horizon I could hear the echoes of gunshots from the valleys below – the day's hunting starts early in the Pyrénées. At first light a strong westerly wind is spinning through the cols and peaks around Organbidexka and for an hour or more carries with it showers of early morning migrants. Keeping low down and working hard across the wind are yellow, grey and white wagtails, tree and meadow pipits and ring ouzels. With them, as the day warms quickly, go swallows, sand and house martins and every now and then a wheatear or two. Small parties of chaffinches and siskins, in search of good seed crops and not travelling far, tumble up the hillside like showers of leaves in the wind and vanish in the woods.

Watching this steady stream of birds, I am reminded of something that T.A. Coward wrote in 1926.

Watch swallows or martins, day migrants, travelling past any particular spot when passage migration is in full swing. We count the stream per minute or per hour, and though the birds do not come in great rushes, we find that the numbers which pass are very large; then we multiply the number of hours during which the migration was noticeable, the number of days, weeks, that it continued, and we marvel. But we forget that at other places in our land and in very many other lands the same or larger streams were passing. What we saw was nothing compared with what actually took place.

Early morning mist rising out of the valleys below Col de L'Organbidexka. A hobby passes through on its way south below some early rising griffon vultures.

Soon the stream of migrant raptors begins to flow past; sparrowhawks, about one every half-hour; red kites, at first just a trickle then waves or five or six passing every 10 or 15 minutes; a few buzzards, a second hobby and a lone honey buzzard. The flow of raptors is interrupted occasionally by an alpine chough or raven passing overhead. Suddenly a goshawk flips into view over the trees further down the hillside and climbing quickly up the valley is over the crest and gone in seconds.

Throughout this time there has been the sound of intermittent gunfire, some of it coming from the hills close by, and each time a shot rings out a jeer rises from the handful of migration watchers and counters gathered on the hill. I had supper with them last night in their observatory, a curious hexagonal dome perched on the lip of the Organbidexka pass at 1347

Swallows and martins over Gibraltar Point.

metres above sea level. It is the base for *L'Opération Organbidexka Col Libre* (OCL), a group that not only monitors the passage of birds through the region, but also fights to end the mass slaughter that takes place here annually.

The Organbidexka is just one of a number of Pyrenean mountain passes. Each pass funnels streams of migratory birds over the mountains and virtually all of them are prized as vantage points by hunting syndicates. The main target in autumn is woodpigeon, but despite being protected by law many other species are shot; hobby, red kite, ring ouzel and even lammergeier. 'They shoot everything', I was told and in the process over a ton of lead is dumped each year on the mountains and pastures of Larrau.

The inter-communal Syndicate of Soule with almost 200 hunters, rents 17 passes in the Larrau valley. In 1979 François Sagot and Joel Tanguy le Gac, two ornithologists enraged by this annual slaughter, decided to try and rent the Organbidexka pass and make at least one 'corridor' safe for migrants. The cost would be 20,000FF per year – 'Operation Organbidexka Free Pass' was born.

Support came immediately from the International Council for Bird Preservation (ICBP), as well as many other conservation organisations in France and other parts of Europe. Just as importantly the group gained support from the local people. They also made great efforts to show parties of schoolchildren how important the area is for migratory birds. In 1985

The passage of swallows and red kites over the Pyrénées at the Organbidexka pass.

pressure eventually led to the French Ministry of Environment deciding to step in and pay the annual rent. Nevertheless, pressure on administrators, politicians and law enforcement authorities has had to be maintained because the illegal killing still goes on.

I am sitting at my easel high on the slopes behind the observatory when one of the OCL people approaches. I did not know it, but for the past hour he has been out on the surrounding slopes collecting a few of the day's corpses to highlight the discussion we had last night about the senseless killing. As if I needed convincing of the tragic futility of the hunters actions, he has brought me a handful of dead swallows. If the pressure is kept up by organisations like OCL, perhaps one day migrants will be given a 'free pass' over the whole length of the Pyrénées.

France is not the only country where birds are persecuted. The passion to kill anything that moves is found also in parts of Portugal, Spain, Italy, Malta, Greece, Cyprus and the Lebanon – in fact, most countries bordering the Mediterranean and presents a formidable and indiscriminate barrage of firearms, lime-sticks, spring-traps, snares, trammel nets and even a few mist nets.

Years ago hunting in these regions would have been part of a traditional subsistence way of life, but there can be very few places now where hunting is indispensable. Today the birds are killed for a 'laugh' or for sport.

The result of a good morning's 'sport'.

There is legislation to make much of the killing illegal, but it is largely ignored and enforcement is virtually non-existent. However, there are sometimes successful prosecutions of hunting violations and changes in attitude are evident at last. In Cyprus for example, which long had the reputation of killing about 25 million migratory birds a year – more per capita than any other country in the Mediterranean – the Government was forced to take action in 1986 after years of protest, and the number killed has dropped to between four and five million a year.

Migratory birds that must cross international boundaries on their journeys have long been of particular concern to ICBP, a federation of constituent member organisations in many parts of the world. In 1983 ICBP, the World Wide Fund for Nature (WWF), World Conservation Union (IUCN) and International Wildfowl and Wetlands Research Bureau (IWRB) launched a Migratory Birds Programme. Coordinated by ICBP it is supported by committees in different countries whose aims are to educate, raise funds and continue to apply political pressure for tougher laws and law enforcement. The slogan of the British committee is 'Stop the Massacre', in Malta it is 'Save the Migrants'. The campaigns have had a number of successes, in countries like Spain, Italy, Malta and France, but elsewhere the situation for the safe passage of migrants remains deplorable. A recent estimate by ICBP put the annual slaughter at at least 1000 million birds.

Many small migrants surviving the journey through southern Europe face another danger as they cross the Mediterranean; but this time the hazard is natural. Cap de Formentor is a ragged peninsula of sharp mountains and towering limestone cliffs that juts into the Mediterranean from the northeast corner of Mallorca, one of the Balearic islands. The Balearics are

well placed to receive many small birds making their way to Africa each year. Unlike the large soaring migrants, smaller migrants have no need to concentrate during the migration at the narrow sea crossings, such as the Straits of Gibraltar or the 160 kilometres of the Sicilian narrows. Their movements are on a much broader front and they can cross the Mediterranean along its entire 4000 kilometre frontage. Every night during the six weeks of the main autumn migration it is estimated that about 30,000 birds pass over each kilometre of coastline, from Portugal to Turkey.

Most migrants usually depart about 45 minutes after sunset. Flying under clear skies and in calm weather at a speed of about 40 km per hour, the 350 to 480 km crossing will take between 9 and 12 hours, a journey that could just about be completed under the safe cover of darkness. In deteriorating weather, the wind speed and direction begin to affect severely the passage of birds. A steady tailwind of 20km would reduce the journey to between 6 and 8 hours, but the same journey against the wind, could take 24 hours.

Climbing out of Puerto Pollensa on the road towards Formentor in the darkness before an October dawn is a little unnerving. The road climbs and twists, swinging around dizzy hairpin bends with the headlights sweeping through the blackness of pine woods at one moment and throwing the beam far out to sea the next. Half-way along the peninsula the road breaks from its giddy progress for a few kilometres and drops down to the sheltered valley of Casa Veyas.

The night had been still and clear to begin with, but by early this morning the wind had strengthened and shifted. Now at first light it is pulling a low layer of grey cloud in from the sea over the cliffs on the north side of Formentor. During the night countless small migrants will have passed overhead as they made their way southward to Africa. But many other birds, having crossed the coastline of France, or even northern Italy or Spain after dark and perhaps being slowed by unfavourable winds, would still be travelling at dawn. Finding the Balearics below them at first light they would alight to rest and feed until evening.

On either side of the road along the Casa Veyas valley floor are small stony fields and orchards of fig and almond spreading between pine woods and patches of rough open ground. The stone walls dividing the plots have been topped with sticks, posts and wires as an additional deterrent against sheep – a sheltered landscape ideal for resting birds. There are wheatears running over the boulders and stones in the fields. Redstarts flit from branches to the ground and back again, and there is a male pied flycatcher as well. A woodchat shrike watches from a stick on a wall and the trees are busy with willow and Sardinian warblers.

The road out along the peninsula resumes its tortuous twists and turns, sometimes passing through pine and oak woods and past steep scrubby hillsides, or crawling around the edge of sheer cliffs, until it ends by the lighthouse on the tip of Cap de Formentor.

Northern Europe bade farewell to summer a few weeks ago. Now at the end of the first week in October southern Europe is changing seasons. Earlier on the cloud had lifted for a while, but now the greyness has closed in again and the wind is more blustery. It looks like rain.

On the fence wires and rocks around the lighthouse are whinchats and wheatears and in the surrounding scrub large numbers of redstarts and robins. Spilling down the cliffs and holding onto the slightest ledge are clusters of pine and shrubby tangles of lentisc where firecrests call and willow warblers search for insects above the grey-blue waters of the Mediterranean.

The sea breeze rises fast up the cliffs and sliding effortlessly in the crosswinds and blustery updraughts are four or five Eleonora's falcons. They are superbly elegant, very agile and swift flying falcons that are, to my mind, one of the most intriguing and beautiful of all European birds of prey.

I watch them for an hour as they sweep and glide on the wind, sometimes beating hard out to sea with a graceful and powerful flight, then turning to hang high almost stationary on the updraughts. Sometimes they stoop low over the waves beating hard back into wind; then they are chasing and calling, or landing on a narrow ledge of bluff on the cliff-face where they perch for a while to preen. The falcons have about them a relaxed and end of season air.

Eleonora's falcon is the only European bird of prey to breed in the autumn, delaying the raising of its brood so that the growing young can be fed on the predictable flood of small migrant birds that must pass across the Mediterranean on their way to Africa. They have a total world population of about 4500 breeding pairs distributed in less than 100 colonies spaced along the sea-cliffs, islands and remote rocky islets of the Mediterranean, with outposts in the Canaries and on the Atlantic coast of North Africa. The eastern end of the Mediterranean holds the largest numbers; two-thirds of the entire world population are found in the Aegean.

The adults return to the breeding colonies in late March and April and most have congregated there by the end of June. During these early breeding months they feed mostly on larger insects which they catch in the air. They will often travel great distances to favoured hunting grounds where flying insects are abundant.

By late July and early August the serious business of breeding is underway, and by the end of August most of the chicks have hatched. In the early stages after hatching the Eleonora's chick is brooded and guarded by the female, and together they are dependent on the food provided by the male. After 10 days or so the female ceases to brood but remains close to the nest

OPPOSITE
An adult and juvenile Eleanora's falcon on the cliffs of Cape Formentor, Mallorca.

receiving food from the male and feeding the growing youngsters. As the trickle of migrants begins to gather pace, their feeding habits change to preying largely on passing birds.

Around sunrise the colonies are emptied of male birds as the peak hunting period is dawn when many weary migrants are approaching landfall. Stacked high in the early morning sea breezes, and spreading for several kilometres down the coast on either side of the colony, there can be as many as 150 or more Eleonora's Falcons waiting to swoop down on the flood of tired migrants.

Hartmut Walter, the distinguished author of a classic monograph on Eleonora's Falcons, spent a number of years observing them at many sites throughout the Mediterranean and one of his observations from Crete highlights the formidable obstacle that the 'wall of falcons' presents to the hordes of small migrants crossing the Mediterranean in autumn.

> *27th August 1965 (Paximada)*
> *17.00 Three Yellow Wagtails (Motacilla flava) attempt – one after the other – to reach Paximada, flying 0.3 to 2m above the waves. Each time, 5 to 8 falcons chase them, flying either behind or above the wagtails and trying to grab the slow-flying migrants when passing over them. Each wagtail escapes at least five attacks by moving suddenly in a lateral direction. Finally all three are captured before they can reach the safety-promising rocks of Paximada. One wagtail is pressed so hard by the attackers that it falls into the sea four times; once it plainly sits in the water without beating its wings for ca. 5 sec; when it has raised itself out of the water, a falcon captures it right away. It is noteworthy that the falcons avoid touching the salt water.*

Yellow wagtails usually migrate during the day and then roost together at night. This, and the fact that they are relatively common birds, has resulted in the species being one of the most studied migrating birds.

The prey species that are captured vary from colony to colony and range in size from small *Phylloscopus* warblers to hoopoes. In Morocco the

Eleonora's falcons occur in two types of plumage, either light or dark phases. The dark phase birds account for about a quarter of the population.

victims are mostly whitethroats, nightingales, woodchat shrikes and redstarts. During the early part of the breeding season in the Balearics young swifts make up a large part of the diet, and wheatears and redstarts are high on the list later on. In the Aegean the most important species are willow warblers and chiffchaffs, red-backed shrikes, whitethroats and whinchats.

During the autumn breeding season there are a total of about 20,000 adult and young Eleonora's falcons living almost exclusively on small migrant birds. The best estimate is that between five and ten million small birds fall victim each year to the falcons. This annual toll, although perhaps high for certain species travelling particular routes which pass close to falcon colonies, is only a fraction of the total number of migrants bound for Africa. For every bird that falls victim there are thousands of others that will survive. But many other dangers still lie ahead.

Of all the migrants leaving their breeding grounds, half will not return the following spring. They will die for many reasons while making the journey or will fail to survive in their winter quarters. For a young bird migrating for the first time it is a flight into the unknown. In its home territory it will have learned quickly to exploit the familiar surrounds, but these advantages are lost as soon as it leaves. The next few touchdowns will be unfamiliar staging posts and then journey's end in the tropics where it must learn quickly to exploit a new set of circumstances. While making the journey, both adults and young birds might be blown off course and with insufficient fuel reserves their survival would certainly be threatened. There are also many dangers in crossing the Sahara desert. If caught by bad weather there are precious few places where they could find shelter and food. Having survived just one migration a bird will have recognised the suitability of a particular route, be familiar with particular staging posts, and will have learned the adaptations it is necessary to make to maintain itself in the tropical winter home. With each annual migration thereafter it will increase its knowledge of how best to perform the journey – the best guarantee that it will survive another marathon. However, small birds have a short average life expectancy, a year or two at the most, so few get to be experienced migrants.

The hazards of migration are a real threat to the survival of many individual birds, yet it must still be an effective strategy, for it would cease to be a viable option if it jeopardised the survival of the species.

By early October virtually all the young Eleonora's falcons will have fledged, and by the first few days of November the breeding colonies are deserted as the population moves away on migration. Birds from the Canaries and coastal Morocco move northeast around the Atlantic coast of North Africa and pass through the Straits. Moving eastwards in a long arc down through the Mediterranean basin, they cross the Middle East into the Red Sea, where they pass down along coastal Ethiopia and Somalia. It is thought that they then turn inland and cross the Horn of Africa, to reach the coast of East Africa. Although a few birds winter along coastal Kenya and Tanzania, the largest numbers cross the Mozambique Channel to reach their winter home in Madagascar. There they will feed largely on flying insects, sometimes bats and birds, until it is time for the return migration that begins in late February, with a few birds staying behind until April.

It might appear that for migrating Eleonora's falcons, finding their way to Madagascar and back each year would be a relatively simple affair. Just keep the coastline of Africa below and to the right in autumn, and to the left in spring; learning to recognise familiar landmarks and the best place to make a sea crossing.

Clearly, navigational mechanisms used by birds cannot be that simple. What features and landmarks are there to be recognised at sea? What happens when visual references are obscured by low cloud? How, after a journey of many thousands of kilometres, is a bird able to locate the same island and even the same nest that it used the previous summer? Does a bird learn the direction it must fly, or is it born with an instinct to migrate? The annual migration of birds involves such tremendous feats of navigation that the mechanisms which enable them to find their way, with such an extraordinary degree of accuracy, must be far more complex.

On the migratory voyage there are an enormous range of direction finding techniques a bird can use, and one particular method might be more important to one species than to another, but most will combine a variety of incoming information.

Random search, or wandering continuously might eventually lead a bird to a suitable place where it would be safe and profitable to spend a season. But total dependence on random search would however be particularly inefficient as there is no guarantee of finding a safe winter refuge. A great deal of feeding time and energy would be used up in ranging over unsuitable areas. On the return migration in spring there would be a chance of not reaching the traditional breeding grounds where others of your species were congregating. Although not a strategy to depend on exclusively, random search does have a part to play in migration. A flock of garganey for example, on reaching the wetlands of the Sahel in sub-Saharan Africa might find a wintering ground dried out and so be forced to search at random across the Sahel for a suitable alternative.

Another way of 'searching' for a route to migrate along could be by a gradual process of familiarisation, with a bird 'visually feeling' the way along coastlines and valleys, rivers and mountains. The return journey could be accomplished by retracing the route past the landmarks which are familiar.

By a continuous process of exploration and learning, knowledge of the home breeding range could be extended down the whole migration route to include the area around the winter home as well, eventually forming a mosaic of mental maps linking the summer and winter home. Stored away would be details of the best feeding sites and how best to travel between them, the landmarks which identify a particularly favourable site and the spatial relationships between them. But sole reliance on this strategy has disadvantages that would make the journey less efficient than it need be. A more direct route would enable non-productive areas discovered on the outward journey, to be by-passed on the return leg. Also, it is a strategy that is often unusable by the largest number of migrants – those that make their journeys by night. Unless there is bright moonlight or starlight they cannot refer to visual landmarks. The same is true of diurnal migrants that must cross large expanses of open sea and be out of sight of land.

From homing experiments that provided clues about the ability of birds to find the way to known destinations, it was clear that they were using more than simple recognition of familiar landmarks to return. In other words, they could navigate. They could orient their flight path in the absence of landmarks previously known to them. But was this navigational ability gained through instinct or learning?

It was Albert Perdeck whose work with starlings in Holland during the 1950s led to a significant understanding of the respective roles that instinct and learning play in bird navigation.

Each Autumn large numbers of starlings leave the Baltic countries flying southwest into the Netherlands, spreading later into northern France and across to the British Isles. Perdeck captured and ringed 11,000 of these birds, a mix of young and adults migrating together, and transported them 600 kilometres to the unfamiliar territory of Switzerland. There he released the two groups separately. The young birds continued flying southwest on a course parallel to their original flight path, and ended up far away from the normal wintering areas, some even reaching Spain. The adult birds reacted differently. Having some experience of migration they were able to reorientate and headed northwest towards northern France and the British Isles, the usual wintering areas already familiar to them. What Perdeck had

Three common Phylloscopus *warblers, the willow warbler, wood warbler and chiffchaff (above) cover greater and lesser distances during the annual migration. The long-distance migrant of the three is the willow warbler which in experimental conditions shows Zugunruhe more frequently and for longer than both the wood warbler and the chiffchaff. The wood warbler, which travels to the low Tropics, shows less Zugunruhe than the willow warbler, but more than the chiffchaff which covers relatively shorter distances, mostly to Southern Europe and Africa north of the Sahara.*

shown was that young starlings inherit an ability to set a fixed 'compass' course and orientate in a given direction, but experience enables a bird to find its way accurately to a particular or familiar area.

Research into the nature of the 'compass' and the innate orientation ability in migratory birds was carried out by Gustav Kramer, a German ornithologist working at about the same time as Perdeck. He built a very special experimental box, the famous 'Kramer's Cage'. In it he placed starlings for a long period of time in an unchanging and artificial environment. What Kramer noticed was at those seasons when the birds would normally have been migrating, they became restless, showing periodic bouts of hopping and fluttering. He measured the direction of this activity with a series of pressure sensitive perches around the cage. The migratory restlessness, usually known by the German term Zugunruhe, was not random but was strongly directional. In October, when the captive birds would normally have been making an autumn migration, their restlessness was recorded most frequently in the south-west corners of the cage. In Spring, when the heading of free-flying birds would have been northeast, the recorded headings in the cage were also north east.

Later work by E. Gwinner and W. Wiltschko in Germany in the late 1970s revealed links between Zugunruhe and innate directional preference

FINDING THE WAY

A family of young wheatears in northeast Greenland, one still with down attached. On the verge of migrating for the first time, for them finding the way to Africa must depend largely on instinct. There is little evidence that they travel in tightly bunched flocks, but instead move in loose groupings calling in the darkness to stay in contact. This might also help them all maintain the same generally preferred direction. But many birds, including juveniles will travel on their own relying entirely on instinct to see them through. For a young cuckoo migrating for the first time, finding the way to Africa can only be instinctive as their southward migration begins in late August or September, long after the adults have left for Africa.

In many species of geese and swans the adults travel with their own offspring as a family group, linking up with other family parties from the same area and together migrating as a larger flock. In this way the juveniles can learn from the adults to recognise a particular migration route, the best stop-over locations and the most favourable wintering areas. The knowledge gained could readily establish a migratory tradition to be transmitted from generation to generation. But young birds are quite able to make the journey themselves, although their efficiency is reduced when they do.

of birds on migration. They showed bouts of nocturnal restlessness that changed in directional preference. These shifts in orientation coincided with the time of year that the free-living warblers would be making the major course alterations as they travelled to and from the winter quarters in Africa. Their work showed that restlessness and shifts in migratory direction during the journey were controlled by spontaneous seasonal changes in the bird's internal physiology. Long-distance migrants had an inborn migratory urge that was pre-programmed with a directional preference. In other experimental work it has been found that the amount of Zugunruhe a captive bird displays is in proportion to its migration distance. Species travelling to tropical Africa show much more Zugunruhe for longer periods than those wintering in the Mediterranean basin. The bouts of restlessness also reflect on whether a bird in the wild migrates by day or by night, for nocturnal migrants when caged show most Zugunruhe at night and diurnal migrants are most restless during the day.

If in inexperienced birds there is a simple inborn distance and bearing programme that in older and more experienced birds can compensate for displacement and common to both is an ability to orient or determine a fixed compass course, how is directional information perceived in birds? By controlling with mirrors the angle at which the sun entered the 'cage', Kramer showed that starlings could detect compass direction with reference to the sun. Although Kramer's starlings were captive, and the species is not a very long-distance migrant, it was strong evidence that a sun compass existed in birds making it possible to explain the orientation of migrant birds in the wild. Recent studies of an American bird that migrates at night, the white-throated sparrow, has also provided strong evidence that patterns of polarisation in the twilight hours are used by birds for compass orientation. Directional information from the sun could also be obtained by a simple sighting of its rising or setting, for nocturnal migrants begin their journeys shortly after sunset and diurnal migrants depart in the twilight around dawn.

However, sole dependence on a sun-compass that made no allowance for the passage of time would have serious consequences for a migrant bird. If it is to navigate with any degree of success, accurate time-keeping is essential. As the earth rotates through 360° every 24 hours, each hour of the day a fixed point on the equator moves through 15° of longitude, a distance of 1800 km. A migrant setting out from western Europe with a constant inaccuracy of 5 mins in its biological clock would have a longitudinal error of about 100 km east to west by the time it reached the Mediterranean, and would be 150 km adrift by the time it reached the equator. A constant inaccuracy of 30 minutes would make a difference of about 900 km at the equator – an error that would easily threaten a successful migration. A bird on migration, if it is not to fly in a circle, must be continuously altering the angle between the direction of flight and position of the sun as it moves through the sky, therefore it must have a biological 'clock'. To investigate the nature of this internal 'clock' there have been a number of experiments over the years with different species held captive in controlled aviary conditions. This enabled the natural cycles of light and dark to be excluded and replaced by cycles out of phase with the outside world. When artificial cycles of 'day' and 'night' were shifted so that birds were kept either in continuous light, in total darkness or a constant twilight in between, their daily activity patterns persisted, implying that the internal 'clock' was free-running and innate, continuing without reference to outside stimuli.

If a time compensated sun-compass can provide directional information to migrants travelling by day, what is the nature of the compass used by the even larger numbers of nocturnal migrants? Although the celestial movements of the moon and the planets might at first glance appear to be helpful, their apparent motion around the earth is complex and most probably of little use. The focus of research has therefore been on the recognition of stars as navigational aids by exposing birds to the night sky under controlled aviary conditions in a planetarium.

Franz Sauer and Gustav Kramer working in Germany during the 1950s showed that, unlike the sun-compass which had been shown to be time compensated, the star-compass was time independent. The implication being that star patterns, and not star movements, were the primary source of information in the night sky. It was the shape of constellations in relation to Polaris, the Pole Star, which provided the most important clues.

An American, S.T. Emlen working in the 1960s with indigo buntings shed more light on nocturnal navigation by rearing birds from the egg without them ever catching sight of the stars. When the buntings were suddenly exposed to the normal pattern of the night sky in a planetarium, they were unable to orient. It seemed that knowledge of the star map was not genetically transmitted. Other birds reared in a similar way were exposed in a planetarium to a normally rotating night sky. The birds were able to get their bearings and behaved quite normally. Emlen then exposed similarly hand reared birds to a correct night sky, but this time the star patterns were shown without rotation. The birds failed to orient. Finally, he exposed indigo buntings to a rotating night sky, but this time the point of rotation was not the Pole Star but Betelgeuse, a brightish star in the constellation of Orion. When the birds were tested they behaved as if Betelgeuse was the Pole Star. At least for indigo bunting, which is not a trans-equatorial migrant however, it appeared that the innate star-compass was calibrated not by an inherited star map, but rather it functioned by the recognition of the axis around which the heavens appear to rotate. In the wild it seemed that in the time between leaving the nest and undertaking their first migration, a young bird watches the night sky observing the point of least rotation and the relation the apparent movements of the constellation patterns bear to a fixed point in the heavens.

The largest movements of night migrants occur when the skies are clear or partly cloudy, but radar has also been able to show that broad-front nocturnal migrations occur also when the stars are obscured. What other sense could birds be using to navigate in total darkness? Although discussed as a possibility for many years, research work in Germany during the late 1960s produced evidence of a third internal compass being used by birds; a magnetic compass.

Acceptance of the idea of a magnetic compass led to research interest in the mechanisms and physiology of how the birds might be detecting the magnetic fields and the search began for a magnetic receptor. A variety of theoretical possibilities have been advanced; one theory, for example, suggested that molecules in the retina of the eye detect the magnetic field. In other work tiny crystals of magnetite were found to be located in the head of pigeons; was this the receptor of magnetic information?

There are three aspects of the earth's magnetic field that could be used to

An osprey flying through a Pyrenean pass late in the evening. Ospreys migrate during the day, so they must find a safe roosting place before night falls.

obtain directional information. The lines of force have a polarity north to south; they have a strength which is greatest at the poles, and they have inclination; that is they vary in the angle they make with the surface of the earth, being horizontal at the equator, climbing steeper in higher latitudes, to be vertical at the poles. The Wiltschkos and their team in Germany again were pioneers with a series of experiments which tested for polarity or inclination as the major reference. Whitethroats and robins, garden warblers and blackcaps were placed in orientation cages where the vertical and horizontal components of the magnetic field passing them could be altered by a system of electromagnetic coils positioned around the outside of the cages. The birds were tested during periods of migratory restlessness when all visual references to the night sky were excluded.

They showed that birds did not have a sense of 'northness' or 'southness' but rather their geomagnetic inclination compass detects the tilt of the magnetic fields that guide them 'equatorwards' or 'polewards'. How far birds travel down the lines of force, and whether they crossed the equator through the doldrums of magnetic information, is governed by the amount of zugunruhe.

What about the remaining senses that birds have; does taste and smell or aural information aid their navigation in any way? In the mid-1970s came experimental evidence from Italy which indicated that pigeons have landmarks in their landscape which they recognised by smell, but the evidence has been conflicting and informed opinion seems to have agreed to differ. It may be that olfactory clues are not essential to successful navigation, even in pigeons, but are used when available and are just one small part of a wide range of incoming directional information. The same might be true of aural clues where the avian landscape is dotted with acoustic landmarks, another area of research where direct evidence from migrant birds is lacking, but where pigeons have shown that their inner ear is capable of detecting very low frequency sounds. The sound produced by the thunder of waves on a distant shore, jetstreams or the turbulence of air passing over a mountain range for example produce very low-frequency sounds and perhaps could be detected by birds.

There are still many unanswered questions surrounding the mystery of how exactly birds find their way with such extraordinary accuracy. As they make the journey they have a variety of navigational options open to them and it is unlikely that birds rely on a single method exclusively, being able to take readings from a range of available directional information; the sun, stars, magnetic fields, odour and aural clues and each species may vary in its dependence on one particular source of navigational information. In fact there is a surplus, or redundancy of information, where only a small part is tuned into at any one time. It might be that different species have a hierarchy of preferred information varying their dependence on a particular set of compass clues; besides, taking a bearing from a wide range of available information is more likely to produce a reliable estimate of direction than dependence on only one source. Perhaps, in the end, birds will be found to be using senses not even suspected nor yet imagined by human observers.

In his book *Bird Navigation – The solution of a Mystery?* Dr Robin Baker, who for many years has been a leading figure in research of navigational behaviour, wrote that, "...the mystery of bird navigation died a very quiet death, scarcely noticed, in the late 70s and early 80s". To a leading academic I am sure that is true. But an artist trying to express migration visually and interpret the biological story involved, sees things differently. So long as 'my' hobbies keep returning, and with every sighting of a swallow or willow warbler in spring, and with every migrant I see on my travels in Europe or Africa, a real sense of mystery and wonder will always surround a migrant's capacity for true navigation.

CHAPTER SIX

Changing Seasons

Defined in terms of all animal species, migration is 'the act of moving from one spatial unit to another'. In terms of bird migration, the definition is 'the movement of bird populations in predictable directions that occur at predictable times of each year, between breeding, and one or more non-breeding areas'. It occurs in response to population pressures and seasonal changes in food resources, allowing exploitation of different geographical areas at different times of the year. Within the definition lie complex patterns and degrees of migratory behaviour.

The patterns of migration for each species, or of populations within it, are modified by their different ecological needs. Each individual bird is making a different journey and has a different timing for the flight. At one extreme are small scale patterns of movement like those of sedentary tits and finches that in winter will move a few kilometres from their woodland homes to find gardens where the feeding opportunities are better. At the other extreme are the regular and predictable patterns of 'true' migrations where birds flow across continents following the rhythm of the seasons. In between lie more unpredictable and irregular migrations such as cold weather movements, nomadism and irruptions. The true picture is that there are almost as many patterns of migration as there are migrant species.

In autumn, as the multitudes of 'summer visitors' are leaving western Europe and temperate Eurasia, millions of 'winter visitors' – birds from vast tracts of the arctic, northern Europe, and western and mid-Siberia – begin their 'true' long-distance migrations. Huge numbers of buntings, pipits, thrushes and finches, as well as millions of wildfowl and waders head towards the relatively milder winter climate of Britain and Ireland, and the near continent of Europe. At that time migrants bound for tropical latitudes are still heading south; the result is an exciting mix of overlapping seasons and migratory patterns. As T.A. Coward described over 60 years ago:

> *...in late September and early October there is overlapping of summer and winter birds. Swallows and martins passing in endless procession; warblers and finches, even turtle doves and spotted flycatchers, had not all departed, and the so called spring and autumn migrants, season visitors, were still lingering. On the floods, fresh or brackish water, were curlew sandpipers, greenshanks and little stints among the more familiar waders of the shore, and wigeon, teal, shovelers, and other duck abounded on the open broad. Autumn, even when the winds are keen and rain is chilly, is a profitable season for the bird-watcher.*

One of the first family parties of whooper swans to arrive on the Ouse Washes.

It is one of those days in the first half of October when you can almost feel the seasons changing and see the birds reflecting the time of year. It has been bright and dry for the past few days, but this morning the wind turned colder and blustery. Now, in early afternoon, low damp layers of grey cloud are being drawn across the sky above the flood meadows and watery fens of the Ouse Washes. Reeds rustle and tall willows arch in the gusts shedding streams of leaves into ditches and puddles down wind. Wrens rattle away from thick beds of teasel and willow-herb. Small flocks of goldfinches riffle through stands of thistle on the river banks and parties of tits bounce through the almost bare canopy of willows. Robins call in hawthorn thickets and parties of starlings strut about, probing the grass. Lapwing crouch head into wind. The rest of the washes are dominated by wildfowl; the main influx of refugees from the colder continental climate in the east have yet to arrive, but already areas of open grass have gatherings of grazing wigeon on them. There are mallard, pochard and tufted ducks, as well as teal, shoveler, gadwall and pintail in the shallows and out on the open water. By the time they peak later in the winter there will be about 70,000 wildfowl, sometimes more, on the Ouse Washes, among them herds of wild Bewick's and whooper swans.

A few swans are already in; five whoopers were the first to arrive in the evening of September 27th. The first two Bewick's swans came in only four days ago. To me, Bewick's are the definitive winter birds, long distance travellers from arctic Russia. The Washes, with an average winter peak of almost 5000, is one of the most important sites for Bewick's in the whole of the UK.

As I sit watching the swans, a swallow or two sweep by in the wind, and every now and then a sand martin passes as well. On a day that tells of the change from autumn to winter the overlapping of summer and winter birds is clearly visible. The migratory pathways of birds on their way to Africa, and still with a long way to go, cross those of swans newly arrived from the Arctic.

Bewick's swan breeds on ice-free areas across the high-Arctic tundra. The entire population is wholly migratory. Those breeding to the east of Taimyr head for eastern Asia for the winter, and those breeding to the west of Taimyr migrate south or south-west to the Caspian Sea or through the White Sea area and the Baltic to reach their wintering grounds in the coastal lowlands of western Europe. Some reach southern and western France. This western wintering population has been estimated at about 17,000 birds.

The harsh chuckling calls of a flock of fieldfares are a characteristic sound of farmland during the winter months. Of the European winter nomads, fieldfares and redwings are perhaps the most familiar, with individuals that one year might wander to Britain, might next year travel to southern France, Italy, or even Greece.

The whooper swan also has a breeding range which spreads across much of northern Eurasia from Iceland to north-eastern Siberia, but breeds further south than the Bewick's. Most of the whoopers wintering on the Ouse Washes are birds from Iceland, a population that is partially-migrant. Some stay behind for the winter but they will emigrate at any time if the weather should deteriorate too drastically during the winter.

The robin is also defined as a partial-migrant, as it is totally migratory in the north-east of its Palearctic range and largely sedentary in the extreme south. It is impossible to say exactly where the robins on the Ouse Washes today have come from. Most of the breeding population in Britain stays within a short distance of their summer territories, although a small proportion move south and south-west into continental Europe in winter, sometimes reaching the south of the Iberian peninsular. In late autumn, mostly during October, large numbers of robins from Scandinavia reach the east coast of Britain and swell the wintering population; many remain for the winter, but the largest numbers move on through France to winter in southern Iberia.

With a breeding range stretching right across northern and central Europe eastwards into Asia, lapwings are mainly migratory in those regions where the winter weather is usually quite severe, and they are partially migratory in areas where winters are milder. It is a species that can withstand cold weather but not prolonged freezing and is perhaps the best example of a bird which frequently performs hard weather movements.

The warmer waters of the Gulf Stream that lap at the European Atlantic seaboard and sweep up past the British Isles and Ireland, make the winter weather relatively milder than the interior of continental Europe. As a result Britain and Ireland are particularly important wintering areas for birds, and lapwings are the most widespread wintering wader. In winters without severe climatic extremes there is a population in excess of a million birds. Lapwings need the soil to be exposed and reasonably soft as they feed on the small invertebrates lying on or just below the surface of the ground. When prolonged hard frosts or heavy snow make feeding difficult, they are forced to move on to coastal mudflats and marshes where the ground is less likely to freeze. If a thaw comes quickly they will return within a few days, but if the freezing conditions are prolonged, they will be forced to travel westwards into Ireland, or else flee south across the sea to France and beyond.

In the bitterly cold and prolonged winter of 1962–3 when even the sea on the east coast began to freeze, the British Isles were almost emptied of lapwings, and the Iberian peninsular was crammed full. Although irregular and unpredictable, this pattern of hard-weather migration has been sufficiently frequent in the past for the Spanish name for Lapwing to be *Avefria* – 'bird of the frost'.

Of the species that show eruptive migratory patterns, perhaps the crossbill and the waxwing provide the best examples. Crossbills breed in large numbers in the pine forests of northern Europe and Russia where they feed almost entirely on the seeds of spruce and pine. Sometimes, when the winter food supply is plentiful and the survival rate high, and a successful

There can be no sight more exciting on a dull winter's day than that of a flock of waxwings reaching and twisting acrobatically as they strip berries from a hawthorn or mountain ash tree.

breeding season follows, a large population of birds is crowded into the breeding grounds by the autumn. If there is then a failure in the seed crop, for the trees of a particular area do not provide an abundance of seed every year, so the birds must move on to where the feeding opportunities might be better. Sometimes they will find a neighbouring forest, but in years when the seed crop over a large area fails entirely, they are forced to wander thousands of kilometres in search of the food they need and crossbills irrupt into south-west Europe.

The waxwing is another bird of the northern forests, and in winter they are dependent almost entirely on berries for their food. In years when there is a large population and the berry crop fails, they pour south into continental Europe, often turning up thousands of kilometres beyond their usual range. They search randomly for berries, of hawthorn and rowan mostly, but will also feed on berried shrubs in gardens, city suburbs and parks.

It was two and a half weeks ago on September 23rd, as dawn broke over the Solway Firth, that I watched a skein of 33 Barnacle Geese glide down through the half-light and land at Caerlaverock. The first wave of migrants had arrived from their summer home on Spitsbergen. Mid-morning that same day a second wave brought another 55 birds, and soon after dawn on the following day, another 38 birds. Yesterday saw the last few flocks arriving – another 3000 birds flew in. Now, the entire population of Barnacle Geese from Spitsbergen are here at Caerlaverock – a total of 12,000 birds.

On their southward migration these Barnacle Geese will have first crossed 1000km of the Arctic Ocean to reach northern Norway. Then they will have moved down the Norwegian coast using traditional staging areas where they will have been able to rest and feed, putting on weight prior to the last stage across the North Sea to Britain. Some will have paused as they made their landfall on the northeast coast of England before moving on to the Solway Firth. On the extensive saltmarsh of Caerlaverock National Nature Reserve and the adjacent farmland of the Wildfowl and Wetlands Trust reserve, they will be able to find security and sufficient food to see them safely through the winter.

When the rain stops just before dawn, the low babble and bark of geese at roost can be heard far out on the estuary. As first light begins to show through thin patches and holes in the wet clouds, I make my way down the lane that leads to the saltings, or merse, below Caerlaverock Castle. The lane is a dark and damp corridor of dripping holly and hawthorn, moss clad sycamores and oaks. It is filled with chaffinches, wrens, blackbirds and robins, and from high up in the greyness comes the rattling chuckle of fieldfares passing overhead. Small flocks of curlews lift off the fields noisily as I pass. Halfway down the lane I hear the sound of geese turning to a roar, like

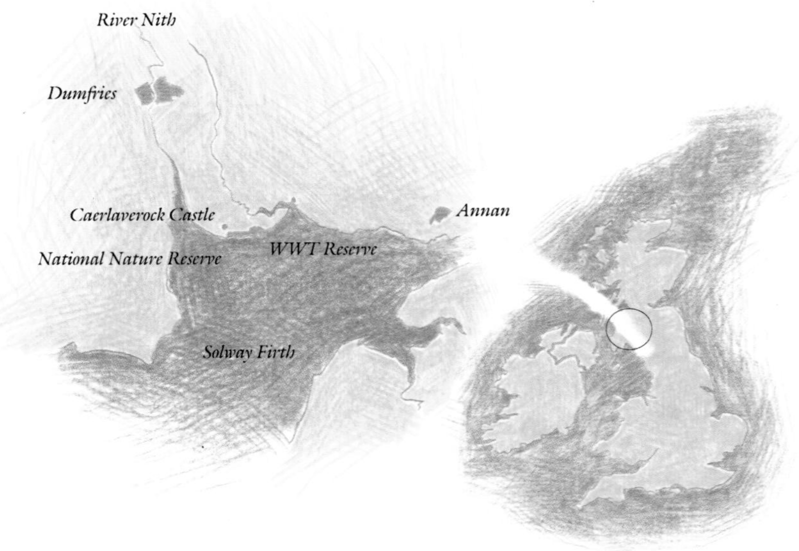

a pack of yelping dogs, as flocks begin their early morning dispersal flights away from the roost out on the estuary.

At the end, where the lane meets the merse, ditches and dark pools filled with willows and reeds run out towards the mud at the edge of the estuary; and beyond there are straggling lines and bunched flocks of geese.

Down towards the mouth of the River Nith, fingers of dryer ground reach out onto the merse from the low banks of the fields along its edges. On these are brambles and gorse, and leaning thickets of hunched hawthorn, shaped by years of exposure to the wind. A stonechat appears on a stem of gorse.

After half an hour watching the flight of geese, it is time to change my vantage point so I follow what I take to be a wildfowlers trackway that leads out onto the merse between the castle, the sanctuary and the reserve. Slowly the sun gains in strength and the cloud lifts a little and as the wind slackens the landscape begins to dry out a bit. The day is beginning to show promise of better things.

I set out my 'studio' between winding strings of bundled grass, plastic

Distant barnacle geese and a peregrine on the Nith estuary. Peregrines in Britain are largely non-migratory, but some wander, or peregrinate, into lowland areas. Estuaries are favourite winter haunts.

litter and seaweed where linnets and meadow pipits are feeding in the debris of the tides. Three hunched carrion crows are perched on a line of fallen fence posts and beyond them a flock of barnacle geese are feeding. There are curlew out here as well, and across the huge expanse of mud there are many dunlin and oystercatcher.

The breeding population of golden plovers on the upland moors and peatlands of Britain and Ireland is about 30,000 pairs. During the winter months they are joined by birds from Iceland, Fennoscandia and northern USSR, taking the winter population to between 200,000 and 300,000 birds

I look up and turn round when a curlew cries calls, and see a peregrine is sweeping fast over the merse. Dropping to within a few feet of the ground it soon rides high again and glides up into wind. Immediately the three carrion crows, already calling noisily, take to the air and attempt to chase the peregrine, but it is too fast. More curlews rise up in alarm. Lapwings and oystercatchers stream up into the air in alarm as well, but as the peregrine sweeps past the feeding geese, their heads go up and they become more noisy, but none fly off. I find the peregrine again quickly and keep it in telescope view as it turns and comes back down the edge of the estuary, skimming fast and low over the rippled sand and muddy creeks. Moments later there is a tumble and a flash of white as a wader falls victim to the peregrine's patient patrol.

In the early afternoon, an hour or so before high tide, I move again, this time further round the merse towards the estuary of the Nith. The cloud has thinned now into soft drier looking bundles that are running slowly down the wind, with glorious autumn sunlight pouring through the widening

A FLIGHT INTO CONFLICT

A flock of brent geese over Old Hall Marshes on the Essex coast. Almost 100,000 brents now winter around the south and east coasts of Britain, from the Humber to the Exe, but their numbers have not always been so high. Following an outbreak of a disease that killed off their traditional food supply of eel grass and green algae, their numbers dropped to only 16,500 birds in the mid- 1950s. Protection from hunting pressures has played a part in their recovery, but so have changing feeding habits. Other saltmarsh vegetation became important in the winter diet, but more significantly they began exploiting grass and cultivated crops such as barley, wheat and oilseed rape. This increasing use of agricultural land has inevitably brought the birds into conflict with farmers. The problem is not whether there is damage, there is, but the scale of the losses. Although one coastal farmer in Sussex has estimated his financial losses at between £5000–8000 a year, yield losses have been shown to be less than 10%. Scaring tactics, such as bangers, humming tapes, shrieking mechanical scarecrows, shotgun patrols and hawk-shaped kites, have all become less and less effective.

There have also been calls for the brent to be restored to the 'quarry list' of species allowed to be shot by wildfowlers. However, it is likely that this solution would create as many problems as it was attempting to solve. Constant shooting disturbance on saltmarshes and estuaries would push more birds on to fields inland. Besides, two or three consecutive and disastrous breeding seasons could put the population under severe pressure when they arrived here to spend the winter.

There is one solution, however, that has been tried and seems to work well, and that is safe refuges. An experimental refuge, established on Thorney Island in Chichester Harbour on the south coast of England, has been very successful. The grass is cut to a length of about six inches, to resemble emerging winter cereals and the birds have been drawn away from damaging neighbouring commercial crops. There is also a scheme involving payment of goose grazing grants to farmers as compensation for setting aside fields, but the sum is not considered enough by most farmers. The conflict continues.

The view towards Caerlaverock from Stanhope with skeins of barnacle greese on the move towards their roost.

spaces in between. Huge pools of light and shadows of clouds are moving slowly across the mud of the estuary below, and although for the time being the wind has died away, along the southwest horizon lies a stack of cloud that is dark and full of rain.

The rising tide is pushing huge numbers of oystercatchers into a massive roost along the seaward edge of the merse in front of me, and across the estuary itself, where the channels are flooding and the mud being covered, there's the constant movement of wader flocks shifting ahead of the rising tide.

Geese are everywhere, with waves lifting off from the fields and saltings and moving around the estuary or heading inland over the hills and fields. All around skeins of barnacle and pink-footed geese are drifting out towards the Solway; some coming down the Nith and others moving out from the inland fields. In the distance I watch through the telescope as a huge flock of barnacle geese gathers in a creek at the edge of the merse out beyond Caerlaverock Castle. It looks like a pre-roost assembly; many appear to be bathing, preening and drinking in preparation for the night they will spend at roost out on the estuary. As the wind strengthens and the cloud builds again behind the hills, smothering the glow of evening light, the flock in the creek begins to break up. First they leave in loose strings of 20 or 30 birds, then all at once, with a roar like a distant cheering crowd, all the others take to the air. It is a thrilling sight. I want to be in a better position to paint this evening flight, so tomorrow I will move to a different vantage point. If the weather is fine in early afternoon, I will try my luck from Stanhope on the eastern side of Caerlaverock.

CHAPTER SEVEN

Chasing the Sun

As the seasons change from summer to winter across Eurasia more than a quarter of all the breeding bird species are on the move. By far the largest numbers are heading for Africa. The total numbers of birds involved are absolutely astronomic. There are estimated to be 900 million willow warblers, 375 million sand martins, over 200 million swallows, 120 million wheatears and 70 million yellow wagtails on the move in the autumn. Travelling with them will be hundreds of millions more from a host of other species of warblers, waders, wildfowl, falcons and larger birds of prey. The best estimates for the total number of migrant birds moving to Africa for the winter were made by R.E. Moreau. After almost a lifetime of ornithological study in Africa, he spent the last years of his life gathering together as much information as he could about the systems of bird migration between the Palearctic and Africa. Reg Moreau's final figure, that took no account of waterbirds such as ducks, waders, gulls, terns and storks, was a total autumn departure of 5000 million birds.

The first sprinkling of Palearctic migrants arrive in Africa in August, with the largest numbers arriving in September and October, and the stragglers turning up in November. The immigrant bird populations from the Palearctic have about 20 million square kilometres south of the Sahara into which they can disperse. The reception area is made up of habitats that range from lush rain forests at sea level to the cold montane vegetation with a continuous succession of moist and dry seasonal savanna lands in between. The key to the ability of the African landscape to absorb such vast numbers of migrants are the seasonal rains which bring about an abrupt and abundant season of berries and insects.

In Africa, spring, summer, autumn and winter are meaningless. South of the Sahara the seasons are determined by cycles of wet and dry, where the most important factor is their duration and intensity which vary greatly with latitude.

One characteristic of the seasonal rainfall patterns brought about by the movement of the Inter Tropical Convergence Zone ICTZ are broad latitudinal bands of vegetation. Each a distinctive habitat type that varies with topography and the amount of annual rainfall it receives. These divisions are particularly apparent in the northern tropics, but in the south they are fragmented by topography. Straddling the equator are areas that remain almost permanently under the rainfall bands. Rain falls almost daily in the lush evergreen forests of the Zaïre basin and on the coasts of Sierra Leone,

THE INTER TROPICAL CONVERGENCE ZONE

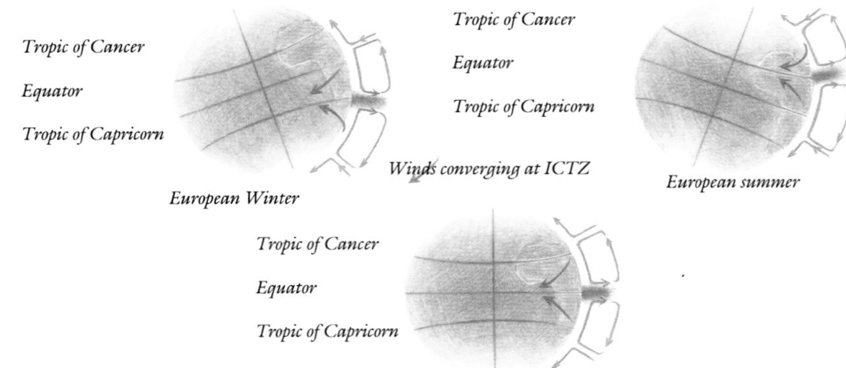

Spring and autumn equinox

The rains in Africa fall as a result of the seasonal migration and pulsation of two air masses. Warm south-westerly maritime air meets dry continental north-easterly air and where the two air masses collide, rain falls. The place where the air masses collide is known as the Inter Tropical Convergence Zone, or ITCZ, and covers a broad latitudinal band.

The ITCZ, carrying high pressure belts to its north and south, oscillates across the Equator between the Tropics of Cancer and Capricorn twice a year. At the spring equinox, the ITCZ moves north across the equator bringing rains to the northern tropics and reaches its zenith at the Tropic of Cancer in June. The amount of rain falling both decreases and begins later, and also ends sooner, the further away from the equator that the zone penetrates. At the autumn equinox the ICTZ crosses the equator again, taking the rains to the southern tropics and by late December the belt of rain lies at its maximum southward advance, over the Tropic of Capricorn where the diminishing rainfall pattern is repeated.

Ghana and Nigeria. The lowland forests are bordered by a transitional zone or Forest Savanna Mosaic, a woodland savanna with patches of moist forest and grassland. This mosaic would at one time have been covered with moist forest, but annual burnings and stock-grazing activities keep it open. Beyond the rain forest is the Guinea Savanna zone, a broad belt of moist woodlands and wooded grasslands lying between about 8° and 11° north of the equator, and between about 10° and 16° in the south, where they are more often referred to as Miombo woodland. The Guinea Savannas have a rainy season lasting about seven or eight months and are characterised by open broad-leaved semi-evergreen or deciduous trees. The open and more airy canopies allow grasses to dominate the ground layer, although shrubs are common too. The grassy areas of the zone are frequently burnt, both by man and by naturally occurring fires during the dry-season. The trees are characteristically thick barked and largely fire resistant. The grasses are mostly deep rooted, thus protecting them from flames and allowing green shoots to appear soon after the grass is burnt.

Beyond the Guinea Savanna lie the drier woodlands and wooded steppes of the Sudan Savanna which includes the Sahel along its northern edge. The Sudan Savanna occupies a belt from about 11° to 13° in the north, but south of the equator it is a less distinct habitat zone being more fragmented by topography. The rainy season lasts for five or six months, and the landscape is characterised by small and shrubby trees that have small leaves to

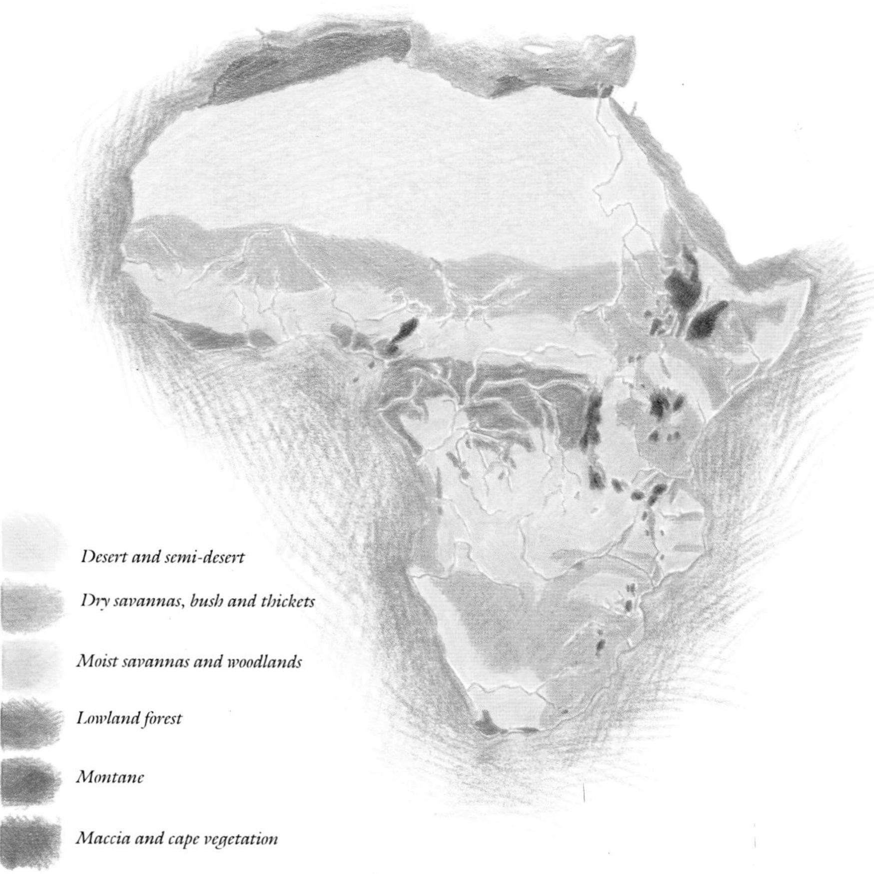

The vegetation zones of Africa.

reduce moisture loss. The trees tend to occur singly and most are *Acacia* species, although the baobab is particularly conspicuous. Grasses, which are shorter and less tussocky, shoot just before the rains. The Sahel or Semi-Arid zone is more lightly wooded and the trees are quite widely scattered, and the grass is short. Beyond the seasonal savannas lies sub-desert, which is characterised by erratic rainfall and low growing perennial plants, ephemeral grasses and herbs, and a few acacias. Finally, beyond the reach of seasonal rains, is true desert, like the vast expanse of the Sahara north of the equator, and the smaller, but equally harsh Namib and Kalahari deserts in the south.

Although these major vegetation zones are marked by relatively smooth lines on vegetation maps of Africa, there are in fact extensive transitional zones and in many areas there are complicated mosaics of different habitats. Together these intergrading habitats cover about a third of the total area of sub-Saharan Africa. The broad latitudinal vegetation pattern is also complicated by interaction of topographical and climatic factors. In the east of the northern tropics the ICTZ moves a greater distance than in the west, bringing two rainy seasons to the seasonal savannas of East Africa. The Ethiopian highlands distort the zones, as do the East African Highlands which

straddle the equator, and south of about 8°S there is an almost continuous succession of high plateaus, mountains, desert and semi-desert reaching almost to the southern tip of the continent.

Cutting through almost every type of habitat are rivers and their associated floodplains. They range from seasonal streams in dry country, to the major waterways of Africa; the Zambezi, Congo, Nile, and the Niger. Scattered in the vegetation zones are wetlands ranging from ephemeral pools lasting only a few days, to the vast swamps of the Okavango delta in Botswana, the Bengweulu swamps and Kafue floodplain in Zambia, the Sudd, Lake Chad and the Niger inundation zone in Mali.

The patterns of dispersal and eventual distribution of the newly arrived migrants into their winter home are sometimes as complex as the patterns of migration that take them to Africa. They show a variety of nomadic, itinerant and sedentary behaviour depending on their habitat requirements and the food available to them. Storks and raptors for example will often follow swarming ants, termites or locusts and in doing so wander over many degrees of latitude. On the other hand it is quite possible that a nightingale will be heard singing in the same location for a month or more before moving on and taking up another territory further south. Some species like the turtle dove penetrate only as far as the limits of the dry northern savannas and Sahel regions. Others like the wheatear can be found wherever there is suitable habitat for them from Sénégal and Mauritania to the Cape of Good Hope.

In general, Palearctic migrants seek habitats in Africa that are broadly similar to those that they occupy in the northern breeding seasons. The notable exceptions are those species inhabiting northern woodlands in summer, which do not use the blocks of evergreen rain-forest. With almost continuous rainfall, evergreen forests do not alter their general appearance from one year to the next and their ecology changes little. Their breeding bird populations, being mainly sedentary, have favourable opportunities at any time of the year. If it is supposed that the number of resident birds in the forest is limited by the food supply and habitat, then visiting migrants would be unable to find either an unexploited habitat or surplus food which they could take advantage of for four, five or six months each year. However, the Palearctic species most frequently associated with gallery forest, forest clearings and edges are pied flycatcher, wood warbler and honey buzzards, but they rarely penetrate the interior. Most migrant insectivorous birds from woodland and forest habitats in Eurasia find a winter home in the huge range of tree and shrub habitats of the seasonal savannas.

At first glance it might appear that the arrival of such large numbers of migrant birds would swamp the available food resources, and create a continuously competitive and energy wasteful search for food among the visitors themselves and with the much larger numbers of resident birds. It would also seem that migrants would be restricted to ecological niches not fully exploited by residents, and the number of residents would be restricted to areas less frequented by incoming migrants. However, the potential for ecological conflict between them is greatly minimised mainly because the

OPPOSITE
Flying termites are triggered to erupt by the onset of rains and provide rich pickings for hobbies. The main wintering range of the hobby is the southern third of Africa, where they are closely associated with rain fronts, feeding largely on the associated swarms of insects.

The Luangwa River in Zambia in October, before the rainy-season.

incomers are represented in Africa by only a few ecologically similar species. But even where there might appear to be considerable ecological overlap, there is a resolution of the conflict.

The opportunities available to visiting migrants are also affected by inter-African migrations undertaken by residents. Some species make regular north-south movements to and from areas altered by dry or wet seasons, others move with the rains, and some will make sudden unpredictable eruptions taking advantage of temporarily favourable breeding conditions or a sudden appearance of an abundant food supply. But talk of ecological overlap and conflict, or avoidance between residents and migrants, is to imply an artificial divide between them. Increasingly it is being realised that migrants are integral parts of the African avifauna – not alien invaders.

It is almost the end of October. Since the end of March no rain has fallen in the Luangwa Valley in Zambia, but in a few days the first few showers of the rainy season should arrive. Until then the valley will stay veiled in a fine haze of dry-season dust and smoke rising up from months of burning grass fires and wind sweeping across the sun scorched landscape.

The day is cloudless and the breeze is hot. From high on the hills of Kapiri Kamfumu, in the South Luangwa National Park, the view across the

Studies of little bee-eaters, one of the five species of bee-eaters, including the migrant European bee-eater, that occur in the Luangwa Valley.

valley shows a wide expanse of sun-bleached browns and yellows stretching away into the blistering haze along the horizon. The burnt colours are broken here and there by green thickets, and in the distance by a thicker and lusher green line weaving along the valley floor; the line marks the course of the Luangwa river.

High overhead a bateleur eagle sweeps fast and dead straight down the wind, rocking a little from side to side in the turbulence of rising thermals. From the piles of boulders stacked around the edge of the hill small flocks of cinnamon-breasted rock buntings flit about busily and every now and then I can hear the soft drumming purr of a flappet lark carried on the wind. As yet, though, no sign of a migrant.

The Luangwa Valley has a rich mosaic of habitats that hold an exciting mix of native birds, but it also provides winter quarters to many thousands of migrants, and acts as a corridor for others heading further south. The valley runs south-west for about 800 km through Zambia, carrying the Luangwa River to the Zambezi. The river meanders along the valley floor through an alluvial belt averaging 100 km in width. On the more sandy soils is miombo or brachystegia woodland. On the river terraces mopane woodland is dominant and on the floodplain there is a mosaic of riverine vegetation; fig trees and tamarinds and cool groves of ebony, as well as open areas of tall kasensi grass and lofty glades of elegant winterthorns. The Luangwa Valley is one of the great wilderness areas of Africa.

The track down from the Kapiri Hills is little used and poorly-marked, just tyre scuffed rocks and loose stones. Down on the valley floor the heat of early afternoon has driven many of the game animals under cover. In the shade of a tree a lone bull elephant stands motionless apart from the slow cooling fan of its enormous ears. But despite the heat, life in the grass and low scrub is as busy as ever. From all around comes the dry muffled sounds

of snipping scissors, clinking cups, worn springs, whirring fans, hums and buzzes, and what seems to be the clicking of a bicycle freewheeling through the grass. A lilac-breasted roller is perched high above the ground on the stump of a dead tree watching the ground below, waiting to drop onto any of these insect sounds if they should show themselves.

Very few habitats in Africa are made up of natural climax vegetation, most have been altered by a long history of human activity. Forest clearance, drainage, flood control, irrigation and grazing pressure ultimately change the patterns of vegetation which affects many hundreds of millions of migrant and native birds that depend on them.

I follow the track across the valley floor until it reaches the gravel road which runs through the park. Turning left I head for the river where the vegetation is thicker. There are combretum thickets trailing at the base of woodland mahogany, tall leadwoods and magnificent sausage trees which at this time of the year have both the pendulous clusters of deep red flowers and long fibrous pods the size of marrows – the 'sausages' that give the tree its name.

All around me the bush is noisy with the activity of birds; weavers and bulbuls, coucals, barbets and babblers topped by the lazy drone of pigeons and doves. A pair of swallow-tailed bee-eaters, keeping low to the ground, make short feeding flights across a clearing in the trees.

Embedded in the vegetation are the enormous hard-baked turrets and fluted columns of termite mounds. Some have sticks and branches poking from them like half-assembled scaffolding holding them up. A movement around one mound catches my eye and in a moment I am watching my first Eurasian migrant in Africa – a male red-backed shrike!

It was almost three months ago and 8000 kilometres away that I had sat at the edge of a sunny hollow in southern Sweden watching and drawing an adult male and juvenile red-backed shrike. What particularly strikes me is the remarkable similarity between the two habitats. Obviously the light is harsher here, but shade your eyes a little, forget the termite mound and the sausage tree for a minute, and compare the rest of the vegetation. Look at the combretum thicket and remember the brambles; look at the lush green canopy of msikisi and remember the oaks. Listen to the droning of the African mourning doves and remember the late summer calls of the turtle dove. To my eye, it is a good illustration of migrants seeking habitats in Africa broadly similar to those they use in the Palearctic.

The valley floor is dissected by small rivers and streams that flow into the Luangwa, but this late in the dry-season all but the largest have dried to sand and hardened mud banks. In mid-afternoon, on the track out to Luangwa Wafwa, I stop to scan the large expanse of open ground of a dambo, areas of open grassland that follow the drainage lines on the river terraces. As I settle with telescope and sketchbook a pair of white-headed plovers rises up calling noisily; a sharply repeated piping call reminiscent of the European oystercatcher. Further out on the hard-baked ground is a small group of waders; long-distance travellers from the steppes of Central Asia and my second Palearctic species – Caspian plovers.

They are slim and extremely elegant birds, about the size of a ringed plover but longer legged and more pointed in the wing. After the breeding season, they will have wandered the steppes in small flocks. This will have gradually merged into the full autumn migration, when they fly high and almost non-stop across the Middle East, arriving on the Red Sea coast of Africa from mid-August onwards, with the main arrivals coming in September and October. Once in Africa they seek short grasslands with sparse shrubby vegetation, gradually shifting southwards, taking advantage of local dry-season conditions. Occasionally they gather together into very large numbers in some particularly favourable areas. Perhaps this small flock is on passage to quarters further south, and when the rains come they will move on.

It is now early November and over a week since I first arrived in Africa. The tufts of cumulus that have been building through the day have now at dusk become stacked into dark thundery heaps against the dusty blue sky. Flashes of lightening soon begin stabbing through the clouds, but no rain falls. Showers are imminent, but storms and the persistent downpour of the 'rainy-season' will come later in December and January.

The Luangwa River cuts a tortuous course down the valley. After the heaviest rains, flood waters in the river wash and slice away the outside bends depositing the silt and debris within the loops. Eventually the river cuts a new course across one of these meanders and an ox-bow lagoon is formed. Abandoned by the river, in time the lagoons silt up and become choked with aquatic vegetation. In time a thin belt of thick woodland en-

Sketches of jacanas, or lily-trotters, and common sandpiper at a lagoon in the Luangwa Valley. It is the constant recurring theme of 'familiar' species from 'home', like the sandpipers, living alogside residents, such as the jacana, that is always visually exciting.

velopes some of the older lagoons, and they become one of the most distinctive and ecologically important features of the valley.

In late afternoon I watch the birds come and go around Mfuwe lagoon; cisticolas and prinias, a crested barbet and a bearded scrub robin, and a small party of melba finches coming down to drink. Jacanas strut about on the floating mats of 'Nile cabbage' turning over leaves and clots of vegetation and picking crustaceans, nymphs or molluscs lurking underneath. A fish eagle lands in a tree at the far end of the lagoon and calls – a shortish series of descendant yelps. Then out of sight, beyond the trees fringing the river, its call is answered. With sights and sounds like these in this hot and richly coloured landscape, the Luangwa Valley to my mind is the heart of Africa with the call of the fish eagle the sound of its soul.

But in a while, I begin to hear snatches of song that in an instant adds a touch of Europe to this African paradise. Somewhere on the other side of the lagoon a willow warbler is singing.

The arrival of willow warblers back on the wintering grounds is often announced by song, and they will continue to sing until about mid-December. Then there is silence until early February when they are heard again, becoming more frequent up to their time of departure. The period of silence coincides with a unique second complete annual moult. Without flight and tail feathers for part of that time they are vulnerable to predation. Remaining silent makes them less conspicuous and increases their chances of survival.

Singing on the wintering grounds has other advantages for migrants. As on the breeding grounds it enables the bird to establish and defend a territory. Where the feeding is particularly good, singing will also ensure that territories are well spaced with little or no overlap, and thus little competition for food.

Another strategy which increases the chance of a migrant surviving the winter in Africa is recurrence – returning to the same familiar location. If the bird remains in a particular area for one winter, by the time it leaves it will have gained intimate knowledge of that one small patch of ground. If it can find the same area the following year the advantages are considerable; the location of the best feeding areas will be known and there will be knowledge of safe roost sites. From ringing studies carried out on the Kafue Flats in Zambia, the floodplain of the Kafue River, it was found that just under half the migrant marsh warblers returned to the same location in successive years, and most were within 6 metres of the territory occupied the previous year. Before bird ringing showed how widespread is the faithfulness of some birds to the same wintering site, there were some delightful observations which hinted at the possibility. Over 60 years ago, in the garden of Government House at Entebbe in Uganda, Sir Frederick Jackson encouraged a yellow wagtail to eat cake crumbs. The following autumn when a bird with the same predilection appeared, he thought it reasonable to assume that the same individual was involved. At about the same time in Egypt, in a small garden not far from Alexandria, Reg Moreau's wife noticed that a White Wagtail with only one leg turned up in two successive winters.

With difficulty I catch a glimpse of the willow warbler *Phylloscopus trochilus* and even if I had perfect views I could not possibly identify its race. It might be a *trochilus* from western Europe at the extreme of its southern wintering range. Perhaps it's an *acredula* from central, northern Europe taking up a winter territory, or even a *yakutensis* from eastern Siberia en route to winter quarters further south in Africa.

But that sort of detail seems a little irrelevant; and right now I am not too bothered which race it is. No matter exactly where in Europe or Asia it has come from, what is certain is that it will have only just arrived here after a very long and dangerous journey, an impressive enough feat for such a small bird that in an instant has linked two landmasses with just a snatch of song.

CHAPTER EIGHT

Into the Heart of Sunlight

It is dawn on a day early in January, and I am in the Cayor coastlands of Sénégal in West Africa. I have slept on a mat alongside the vehicle with the night air and canopy of stars filtered only through a fine mosquito net. After breakfast of bread, jam and tea I make my way along a track through the sand dunes towards the shore. The smouldering of wood fires in a nearby village during the night has left a thin blue film of smoke floating through the palm groves in the still of dawn. Donkeys have been braying and I could hear talking in the village long before first light as animals were loaded and men prepared for the days work in the cultivated strips and patches spread out behind the dunes below the village. As the sun climbs quickly over the palms the sea breeze begins to stir, clearing the air and bringing with it the sound of heavy surf breaking on the beach on the other side of the dunes. The palms sway lightly in the breeze, their leaves rustling with a dry papery hiss and their fronds swaying and knocking together with a light and hollow tapping sound.

Already the sun is heating up the day. Columns of warm air rising high over the sand draw in a slightly cooler and moister breeze from the sea. High above in the fine breezy mix of dust and salt spray, a flock of lesser kestrels loosely circle. Far out to sea two small fishing boats are working nets in the long Atlantic swell and crowded above them is a mix of terns and gulls. Flying just offshore a small flock of sanderlings flash by, keeping close to the waves. Looking down the wide sweeping curve of rolling dunes and

A whimbrel on the coast of West Africa. It will have stopped in one or two places on its way down from Europe. At each stop they can lay down up to 25% of their body weight as energy rich fat, enough for a non-stop flight of over 3800 km.

sand bars that stretch into the salty mist along the horizon, the beach is deserted, apart from a few whimbrels and a small flock of grey plovers.

I count three ospreys in the haze. Then another bird appears over the palms, gliding on long, angled wings. With a powerful flapping action, it flies out beyond the line of breakers, circles for a while, gradually dropping lower, then turning, with tail fanned, it 'hangs' on the breeze 15 or 20 metres above the waves with loose and heavy wing beats – then it dives. The wings are pulled in close to the body and the legs bunched, at the last moment the legs sweep forward as the osprey plunges into the sea and is lost for a moment in a column of spray. Then it struggles from the water with a fish grasped tight in its talons – it beats its wings hard to gain height, shakes water from its feathers, turns and heads back inland over the palms. In a while it is lost to view.

There is a very high chance that the ospreys in Sénégal include some from the Scottish population. Recoveries of ringed birds have shown that the east to west breeding distribution of European birds is mirrored in West Africa in winter. Birds ringed in Scotland, at the extreme west of their Palearctic breeding range, have been recovered from the extreme west coast of Africa, from Mauritania to Gambia. Swedish birds have been found from Sénégal to Nigeria; and Finnish birds, although overlapping with Swedish birds, appear to spread further east into Zaïre and Gabon with a few recovered as far east as Ethiopia.

Watching these ospreys I am reminded of some of the other sightings I

Ospreys are one of the most specialised birds of prey, feeding exclusively on fish, mainly medium sized fish that live close to the water surface where they are more visible and easily caught with a spectacular aerial plunge. Once caught the slippery prey are held in powerful talons that have soles covered in tiny spikes. Grasping of a wriggling catch is further aided by a reversible outer toe that makes the grip even more secure.

have had in the past few months. Just before they left for Africa, I visited the famous Loch Garten pair so carefully guarded by the RSPB in Scotland. In southern Sweden I watched one fishing at Lake Tåkern in soft evening sunlight. On a hot afternoon some weeks later I was surprised by a bird on migration when it appeared over the spoil pits at the old sugar beet factory at Ely, not far from my home, in the heart of the Fens. A little later, on the Isle de L'Oléron on the Atlantic coast of France I had watched a youngster on its first migration fishing old oyster beds. Only a few days after that had been the sight of an adult bird passing through one of the high passes in the Pyrénées as the evening light began to fail. Piecing these visual fragments together, I have one picture of the osprey as a species chasing the sun, the round of seasons explaining the chase. By moving south as the seasons change they have in effect maintained themselves in a permanent summer season. Arriving in their winter quarters from late September onwards they frequent any suitable aquatic habitat, from sea coasts and estuaries to small pockets of water some distance inland. Meanwhile their summer breeding grounds will be in the icy grip of winter, locking up the water on which the osprey depends for food. To survive they have had to escape the winter.

As the tide comes in during the afternoon, there is a steady build up in the number of terns and waders assembling on one spit of sand that curls from

Osprey hunting grounds in a coastal lagoon at Bald Cape in the Gambia.

the beach into the mouth of a creek further down the coast. After an hour there are over 100 terns; many lesser-crested, some caspians, sandwich, and a few royals. Waders are gathering too; sanderling, ringed and grey plovers, turnstones and a few bar-tailed godwits. Offshore, a string of oystercatchers pass; they are a great surprise for I had no idea that they wintered this far south. A handful of grey-headed and two lesser black-backed gulls join the roost. At high tide there must be over 200 roosting birds spread along the sand, a rich mix of birds from far and near.

It is late afternoon, with a strong sea breeze and high veil of cirrus cloud, when the tide peaks. An osprey, flying down the coast, lands on the beach way beyond the roost. It preens and looks about for a while until two dogs, all saggy teats and chewed ears, make their way out onto the beach. Heads down and sniffing they continue to zigzag down the sand, running into a sudden rising flurry of waders, terns and gulls, and the single osprey.

The scrub and palm covered dunes of the coastlands run parallel to the shore and form a distinct climatic strip, in places up to 50km wide. Here the water table is higher than the adjoining country and, with the addition of moist sea air, the vegetation is more luxuriant than the drier landscape of the interior. Trapped between and behind the coastal dune system are long depressions that are fed by intermittent streams. Some form shallow lakes that have marshy edges and wide muddy margins which are used for cultivation, and there are dense clusters of oil and borassus palms around their edges. Some of the depressions further inland are wider and stretch parallel to the coast for many kilometres and, with little or no standing water, form long dry grassy plains. Lying behind the village of Deni Biram N'Dao are two such shallow sheets of water, separated by a line of marshy vegetation, that together spread for three or four kilometres down the coast behind the dunes. This place is absolutely alive with birds, and by far the largest numbers are migrants.

Working their way into the breeze, hanging and drifting lightly over virtually every patch of aquatic vegetation, are marsh harriers. I count at least eight. Redshanks fly up every now and then calling loudly as they are disturbed by the approach of a harrier. There are large numbers of curlew sandpipers, black-winged stilts and little stints feeding in flocks all round the muddy margins. There are also Kentish plovers, ringed plovers, wood sandpipers and one green sandpiper.

Feeding with these Palearctic waders are two Kittlitz's sandplovers, African waders that are a little smaller and more compact than the Kentish plover. With their bodies stooped forward they run rapidly about, swishing heads quickly from side to side, snatching and scooping and skimming through the swarming flies that billow up like small puffs of black smoke from the mud. A yellow wagtail is also attracted to the fly swarm and lunges and springs at the insect cloud which rises like a bow wave just ahead of the zig-zagging bird.

The trees and scrub that surrounds the water is also alive with the zipping, clicking and rattling calls of finches, bulbuls and cisticolas. Behind the dunes, where the ground rises slightly, thick groves of oil palm straggle a short way out onto dryer grassland with a light covering of thorn bushes. Here and there is the enormous bulk of a baobab tree. A Montagu's harrier skirts an edge of the grassland, as a chiffchaff, working its way through the light canopy of an acacia nearby, begins calling. Another sudden and dramatic link between home and the tropics.

Before the intense heat of the middle part of the day drives me under cover, I sit at the edge of the cultivated plots where Ibrahim, a migrant worker from Guinea, is busy hoeing a small patch of tomatoes. As the dry-season progresses and the water levels in the coastal wetlands fall, more and more of the floating grasses and reeds around the margins are cleared for

A yellow wagtail feeding on clouds of flies.

cultivation. The crops they tend are mostly vegetables: onions, cabbages, aubergines, potatoes and tomatoes grown on very small individual plots and irrigated by hand. When he has finished carrying water, he begins clearing grass below the plot, piling it up ready for burning. Within a moment there is a whinchat perching on the pile and flying down quickly to the ground, then flitting back up to the vantage of the pile again.

The whinchat is a strongly migratory Palearctic species that winters south of the Sahara, mostly in wooded savanna and scrub grasslands. In Africa and on the Eurasian breeding grounds they favour exactly this type of habitat; open rough ground with fences, posts, tall plants and herbage that they can use for look-out perches, dropping down to pick up straying insects, larvae, spiders or small worms from the grass stems.

In a short while some yellow wagtails appear, then a flash of brilliant sulphur yellow as a yellow-throated longclaw dives into the uncut grass just ahead of Ibrahim's machette. They are large, robust pipit or lark-like birds found in most open country south of the Sahara. I had shared a meal with Ibrahim last night and we talked about each other's families and the names of our home towns. But more interestingly, I learned that it was necessary, "to water with chemicals because of bad pests", and that they could get two or three crops a year from a plot.

Yesterday I had seen the corpse of a bird in the distance, dangerously out of reach on the mud. Without knowing the exact circumstances for that particular individual, I know there is a problem in many parts of Africa with the indiscriminate and careless use of agricultural chemicals. Some of them, which are known to be lethal to wildlife and which have been banned in the developed world, are still freely available and widely used in many developing countries. It would be irresponsible and indefensible to ban their use

In Europe and North America it has long been known that the use of organochlorine pesticides can have far-reaching and often catastrophic effects on non-target bird populations. In Africa there have been many cases of bird mortality which have been directly attributed to pesticide use, but little hard data exists on the effects they have on bird populations, particularly on wintering populations. Large quantities of pesticides are still used to control locusts and other crop pests, as well as to control malaria and disease vectors such as the tsetse fly.

The application of pesticides will sometimes be careless, haphazard and indiscriminate. Mixing instructions and proportions might not be clearly understood and measurements of quantities perhaps imprecise. The final mix might also be over generously applied.

There is positive evidence that pesticides are accumulating in African food chains and already the effects can be seen in breeding raptors. Effects can also be seen further afield. Peregrines breeding in Sweden and feeding on trans-Saharan migrant waders still have higher levels of contamination than birds feeding on residents like pigeons. Whitethroats have been caught in Sweden during their spring and autumn migrations and analysed for contamination with chlorinated hydrocarbons. Levels were found to be significantly higher in birds that had just travelled from their winter quarters in Africa, but exactly where it was that they picked up the contamination is uncertain. However, what is certain is that the use of pesticides in countries that lie on the migration routes, or their use in the over-wintering countries, pose a threat to the well being of many species of migrant and resident birds.

as the survival of many livestock and crops depend on their use, but less damaging alternatives are available.

Along the length of the Cayor coastlands a network of dirt tracks and paths weave through the huge dune system. Twenty kilometres north of Deni Biram N'Dao I find a track that runs along the crest of sand hills overlooking a vast sea of grass studded with low scrub and small trees; it is one of the dry niayes. The way down is marked by the silvery sparkle of crushed sea-shells winding into the heat haze below. Blue-bellied rollers, spaced with the apparent regularity of lamp-posts, perch on the tops of broken thorn and palm stumps as they watch and wait to drop onto any small lizard, beetle or grasshopper that comes within range.

The flat expanse of grassland is not completely dry. Along the middle trickles a thin stream of clear salty water, the dry-season's changing water levels marked by white lines of sun dried salt crystals lining its edges. Much of the area seems to be divided up between territorial pairs of spur-winged plovers as they call with every move you make. On the stump of a thorn a black-eared wheatear watches the ground silently. This will be a bird from south-west Europe or North Africa, as that population is known to winter in the belt of semi-desert and dry acacia savannas of Sénégal, south-west Mauritania and Mali. But the most exciting migrants down here are the Montagu's harriers. At one point in mid-afternoon I count five of them in the air at one time, each lightly drifting and floating, wavering on the strong breeze coming in from the sea. I check them carefully for an unlikely, but possible, pallid harrier.

I remember the pair of Montagu's in Norfolk I watched on and off through the summer as they reared their two young, and again I am struck by the similarities of habits. At home the nest site was in a field of oil-seed rape in the middle of a huge flat landscape of mostly cereals behind the sea-wall. Here in West Africa the landscape is an expanse of grassland behind the coastal dunes. The main difference is in temperature; on a hot summer day in Norfolk the temperature might reach about 24° or 25°C, whereas at lunchtime today, sheltered from the wind down in this hollow, it reached almost 40°C.

The Gambia is an enclave, a tiny sliver of a country running for 320 kilometres inland from the Atlantic coast into Sénégal. Not much wider than the lower Gambia river itself, Gambia is one of the smallest countries in Africa. Banjul the capital is situated on two low lying spits of land that curl into the mouth of the river from its southern shore. In years past the town was badly overcrowded and malaria and yellow fever were widespread. The town was frequently flooded and in 1937 likened to, "a water logged sponge, floating in a sea of its own excreta". Fortunately, since then the installation of flood and storm drains, and the building of a bund and road, as well as land clearance and reclamation has made the town healthy again, and congestion has eased. But a remnant of the 'sponge' can still be seen, trapped in a corner behind the back-streets of Banjul and the bund road. A more putrid and fetid patch of land it would

Studies of spur-winged plovers. They occur in a wide variety of habitats, mostly in the Sahel and Guinea zones of the northern tropics, but are seldom found far from water.

be difficult to imagine, but a site more jammed with birds, and large numbers of them from the north, it would be hard to find anywhere in Africa.

I have 'borrowed' an off-duty policeman for a couple of hours to show me a safe way in to the site. The deal is that he stays with me to see me safely out again. A deep ditch of purple black water, choked with rubbish, is spanned by a springy palm plank. We then walk around the dry edge of the 'sponge' and are soon surrounded by a dismal smell and a constant whining hum from clouds of flies. The ground is littered with stacks of human faeces and decaying rubbish of every conceivable description. Streams with the consistency of paste creep silently across sticky mud eventually sliding into the stagnant ooze and pools of open water lying in one tilted corner. I wish now I had brought some long rubber boots. With extreme care I find a spot where I can safely sit on my sketching stool and begin work.

The tide is now high in the Gambia River and the mud flats in the estuary are underwater, so many of the waders have been pushed to roost on this side of the bund. The range of migrant species in such a small area, and so close to the town, is quite extraordinary. Wading deep in the dark treacly water are four avocets and two marsh sandpipers, as well as black-winged stilts, greenshanks and ruff. There are curlew sandpipers, dunlin, ringed plovers and feeding on a muddy strip in the ditch along the side road is a Temminck's stint. Tucked behind a line of reed stems, a flock of 20 or 30 knot are roosting.

The contrasts presented by these knot are the most striking of all the summer/winter images I have seen. I remember the lone female and its two chicks that I watched six months ago in the chilly pristine wilderness of Greenland, and I compare it with this hot and mucky man-made urban corner of Africa. The contrast in the birds themselves are striking too. Gone are the spangled russets and warm tones of the summer plumage, instead they are wearing their much duller and more uniform grey-brown of the winter plumage. With the roosting waders are lines of standing gulls and terns strung out along the slightly dryer ground, and overhead wire-tailed swallows and little swifts sweep through the clouds of insects in the air. On a stem of mangrove, which is sheltered from the breeze but bathed in harsh sunlight, a reed warbler sits preening. Then for a short while, with feathers fluffed and head tilted, it sits soaking up the sun. There are many good ecological and survival enhancing reasons why this reed warbler should have migrated from the Palearctic to reach this particular spot in Africa. But for a moment it looks like the only reason is to enjoy the tropical sunshine.

For a day or two I follow the road inland that winds the length of The Gambia across low sandhills, shallow valleys and through villages mirroring the course of the river, but away from the dangers of flooding and nuisance of mosquitoes. The Gambia River receives most of its water from the mountains in Guinea and reaches its maximum flow at the height of the wet-season in August. Bordering the river is a dense curtain of vegetation, but here and there the river or seasonal floodwaters spill out into open swamps. These swampy habitats are important areas for wintering migrants; among them garganey, pintail, avocet, greenshank, common sandpiper, redshank and spotted redshank.

At Jakhaly Swamp, 270 km inland from Banjul, I find large numbers of migrants and a wealth of resident species – so I linger for a while. It is the early morning of January 14th and as the sun creeps over the swamp, it illuminates an African hawk eagle perched high on a baobab waiting for the sun to start heating and stirring the air to help give it lift. The cooing of vinaceous and laughing doves quickly replaces the night long rasping of cicadas. Grey plantain-eaters start clamouring, and the surrounding scrub is soon busy with coucals, bee-eaters and a host of resident species, including two of the beautiful 'woodland' kingfishers, the grey-hooded and blue-breasted. I stop for a while by a still and milky green creek overhung by dwarf fan palms and choked with tall reeds and mats of floating vegetation. A swamp flycatcher, smaller and darker than the spotted flycatcher but of similar habits, makes circuits from the slatted shadows of the overhanging palms into the harsh sunlight and clouds of insects over the water. A reed warbler, working through the dense vegetation emerges on to an overhanging stem picking insects from the foliage, and moments later retreats in to the shadows again.

Much of Jakhaly swamp is cultivated rice fields; at this time of year some have been harvested and are dry, but others are already ploughed and partly flooded. The area is bordered by thick scrubby vegetation and a network of deep dykes that run down to the river, and is criss-crossed by a network of raised pathways and tracks. On one well worn path two early morning cyclists pass under a Montagu's harrier quartering the fields, and as they disappear into the scrub at the end, their voices and rattling bicycles disturb a lizard buzzard that drops out of a tree and in a fast weaving flight disappears through the bush. A pied kingfisher, perched on a rusty arm of a sluice gate at the end of the path stays put as they pedal by. Down by the river, where a line of rice-fields has been rough ploughed leaving pockets of water in a lumpy expanse of mud and stubble, is where the biggest concentrations of birds are. In one field a flock of over fifty black-tailed godwits are feeding and there are almost as many ruff; with spur-winged plovers as well.

Godwits in their tens of thousands winter in Sénégal and Gambia, and they are common in other freshwater margins and floodland in the northern tropics of Africa during the winter months. Most of the sub-Saharan wintering birds are from the west or central European and west Siberian population. At about 20°E, roughly marked by a line through Europe from Greece to Finnmark, there is a 'migratory divide' where the population to the west migrate to West Africa, and those to the east move to eastern central Africa.

Progress inland through the Gambia is slow. The road surface is poor and there are few signs to help. Between villages the road winds on through an open savanna that is a parkland-like mix of shrubs, grass and tall trees, but by the time I reach a few kilometres beyond Fatoto, where the Gambia River runs into Sénégal, a change is clearly detectable in the landscape. The change marks the transition from Guinea Savanna to Sudan Savanna. The crumbling tar-sealed road ends suddenly and a dusty brick-red dirt track winds on through a more open, gently undulating grassland. There are fewer trees and more isolated shrubs, and thicker more tussocky grass. Villages are now more widely spaced, and each one is surrounded by the sharp tangled litter of harvested millet, and by cultivated plots fenced with thorns. It is a landscape of weavers and hornbills, fire-finches and glossy starlings, as well as being busy with migrants from the far side of the Sahara; redstarts, wheatears and black-eared wheatears being the most visible.

Heading northeast across Sénégal, from Tambacounda to Kidra, progress is slow with no roads, just tracks through the bush. Over a number of days, the crawling pace of the journey makes the gradual change from Sudan Savanna to the semi-arid Sahel more easy to detect. Light woodland and acacia scrub grows gradually thinner and the ground becomes more stony or 'cobbled' between the grasses. Villages change from a loose assembly of huts with conical roofs of straw to more compact gatherings of squat mud buildings with cool dark interiors showing through open windows and doors. Redstarts are still common and wheatears too, but there are whitethroats, woodchat shrikes, and the first pallid harrier I have seen on the journey so far; a mature adult male drifting low across the hot and dusty breeze, the characteristic black wedge on the outer primaries contrasting in the harsh sunlight with the pale grey almost white of the uppersides.

These changes in birds, vegetation, and the look of the landscape are not only of academic interest. As an artist on migration it is important that I do not pass through without noticing them. Most of the species that migrate to Africa winter in the northern tropics and a majority of these remain in the dryer Sahel and Sudan Savanna regions. It seems that the Sahel in particular is one of the most important mechanisms in the Palearctic-African bird migration system. Like a chain it links the cycle of seasons in temperate

Eurasia with sub-Saharan Africa. But there are paradoxes in its ability to maintain this vital link.

In September and October the short wet season is ending as the Palearctic migrants start arriving in even larger numbers south of the Sahara. With the onset of the dry season the effects of dessicating heat, termites, wind, natural de-foliation and grass fires make it appear that the landscape gradually deteriorates for the duration of their stay and there will be no remission until the migrants have departed again for the north. At the same time, on the far side of the equator, the rains are about to start as the birds arrive and they will hardly have ceased by the time they depart in March or April. It might be supposed therefore that, although the dry wooded steppes of the Sahel and lightly wooded Sudan Savanna are the closest usable vegetation zone available to migrants, they would avoid those zones and instead pass over into the moist seasonal savannas south of the equator. The reality, of course, is the reverse. But not only can they maintain themselves for six or even eight months, at the end of their stay they are still able to find enough food to fuel the long journey home. How the Sahelian ecosystem is able to resolve what is known as 'Moreau's Paradox' is by a complex web of feeding strategies and migratory patterns in both immigrant and resident bird populations.

The cycle of flowering, fruiting and leafing in a whole range of shrubs and trees are equally significant. Many flower during the dry-season and harbour a considerable insect fauna. There are also a number of evergreen or semi-evergreen species of trees and shrubs in the Sahel, including *Balanties aegyptiaca* and *Salvadora persica* or saltbush, which produce an abundance of fleshy sugary fruit which many insectivorous migrants switch to feeding on. The importance of the Sahel is even more pronounced in the spring when many species that passed through it on their way south reappear on passage and stop and feed before continuing north.

Without a close look at the workings of the Sahel myself, it is clear that my story of migration will not work either. But I will come to that in detail later. There is another intriguing and important aspect of this dry and fragile Sahelian landscape that is particularly fascinating. Again, paradoxically it provides a variety of wetland habitats, some of which are among the largest wetlands in Africa, such as Lake Chad, the Sudd, and the inland delta of the Niger river in Mali, all of them vital to huge numbers of wintering Palearctic wildfowl. The image of vast seasonal wetlands sprawling across the semi-arid heart of the Sahel is a contrast I cannot resist as an artist. As a 'birder' I cannot resist either the opportunity of witnessing some of the largest concentration of birds in Africa. To put together a complete story of migration I have to get into one of these enormous wetlands. So, leaving Nioro du Sahel at the end of the second week of January, I am heading east across Mali towards the sprawling inland delta of the Niger river.

CHAPTER NINE

The Fragile Flood

The Niger River passes through almost every climatic and vegetation zone in West Africa on its 4200 kilometre journey from its source to the sea. Rising in the highlands of Guinea, only 250 kilometres from the coast, the river runs northeast, away from the sea, for a third of its length to the edge of the Sahara desert at Timbuktu. There it turns southeast over the long 'Niger Bend' pushing its way through sands at the desert's edge to flow on for a further 2000 kilometres to the Gulf of Guinea and its sprawling delta in Nigeria.

In former times, when the climate and vegetation of Africa were very different, the upper Niger flowed into a vast inland sea called Arouane, an area that is now an arid plain of dunes and rocky outcrops lying in semi-desert. Reminders of those ancient sand choked waters still exist in the inundation zone, or inland delta of the Niger river in Mali. Every year seasonal flood waters from the river spill onto a vast and uneven floodplain creating a vast mosaic of dry land and wetland habitats that vary from shallow muddy pools and huge lakes choked with vegetation, to completely flood-free areas; the extent of each depending on the amount of water they receive. Twenty or thirty years ago the maximum area of flooding in this inland delta was about 25,000–30,000 sq km. In recent drought years however, the annual flood has fallen and now covers only about 4000–5000 sq km. Nevertheless, the inland delta is still one of the most important wetland areas for wintering migratory birds in West Africa.

A Sahelian landscape with baobab near Simi at the edge of the inland delta of the Niger river in Mali. The baobab is sometimes known as the 'upside down' tree because it appears to have its roots in the air.

After the rains of June, July and August a multitude of ephemeral pools and seasonal streams are left behind in the Sahel surrounding the delta. They carry not only a mass of seed from grasses that have grown over the 3 month rainy season, they will also be alive with invertebrate life triggered into multiplying by the rains. A rich supply of food is available from about September onwards, just at a time when arriving water and wildfowl numbers are rapidly building up. As the dry-season progresses through September, October and November and the rain-fed pool systems slowly vanish, the flood in the delta is rising and by late November it reaches its peak. As the flood subsides it too leaves behind a mass of plant food from aquatic grasses like bourghou that seeded in the rising water and a vast supply of invertebrate food is available in the mud and shallows. Now, ever increasing numbers of migrants head for the inland delta and in January they reach their peak; almost 200,000 ruff, about 50,000 black-tailed godwits, over 200,000 pintail, and almost a million garganey – which, for that one species, is about a quarter of the total world population.

However, the rains are neither regular or predictable and sometimes they fail altogether. Between 1980 and 1983 the flood in the Niger delta grew worse every year, culminating in 1984-5 in the lowest levels of water ever

Studies of black-tailed godwits and glossy ibis feeding in the shallows of Lake Debo at the heart of the inland delta. The godwits are migrants, but the ibis is both a migrant and a resident species in Africa.

recorded. This was the year that also saw the enormous human tragedy unfold in Ethiopia.

These annual changes in the amount of floodwater reaching the delta seriously affect the extent and duration of the flood, two factors that are particularly significant to birds. Reduced flood area effects the availability of food, and flood duration is critical in supporting migrants at the end of their stay when they need to store enough 'fuel' for the journey north.

But it is not only birds that are dependent on the delta and its variable annual life-giving flood; over 500,000 people depend on it too. There are wetland rice cultivators, millet farmers on the dryer land, fishermen, and transhumant pastoralists who herd over one and a half million sheep and goats and over a million head of cattle into the delta.

Long before the present cycle of drought began, the floodwaters of the Niger were thought of as being 'wasted' simply because they were not being 'used' for irrigation and hydro-electric power generation schemes. In fact, the waters have for at least a few thousand years or more been 'used' extremely well to power a large and extremely complex ecosystem.

Since the early 1940s, when the first large scale irrigation dams and barrages were installed on the Niger, the impact of upstream water management systems on downstream ecosystems has never been written into the equations, but the proportional impact of one on the other is huge. Already in Mali there are three dams and more are proposed for the Niger, as well as the Bani River which feeds water into the south east corner of the delta.

An ecosystem functioning sustainably to the advantage of the people that depend on it, must also be to the advantage of birds – a harvest of bourghou grass on its way through the delta by pirogue.

All this, despite the fact that man-made drought is already a factor in the deepening spiral of destruction of the Sahel.

Against the background of current drought conditions, subsistence farmers, fishermen, and pastoralists have little choice about how they exploit their environment. Traditional rice growers, dependent on the natural flood to get a crop, have had to move their sowings further and further out into the delta, bringing them into conflict with transhumant pastoralists who traditionally graze their herds there. Areas that have the potential to flood have received no water for years, so a range of habitats previously available to birds and people has vanished; large areas of *Acacia nilotica* woodland which requires flooding each year has been abandoned by the flood and died completely. Other areas of acacia woodland have been gradually destroyed by abusive grazing practices and extensive cutting.

With such large numbers of Palearctic and Afrotropical birds dependent on the inland delta, the International Union for Conservation of Nature and Natural Resources (IUCN) have taken a great interest in the area. Because the bird populations and human subsistence activities were so closely linked in exploiting the same environment, and both were dependent on the same variable water levels, the emphasis of their work has been on development based on the use of natural resources.

The work of IUCN concerned itself with the better management of the remaining resources and the need to build them up. They learned from the people how they used their land, then encouraged self-help schemes that showed how they could actually do something to offset the worst effects of the drought. They also make annual aerial counts of the numbers of waterfowl supported by the wetlands. Their work has resulted in the replanting of *acacia* woodland, encouraging an increase in the breeding numbers of some of the colonial tree-nesting birds like spoonbills, egrets and storks.

Red-throated bee-eaters and a gonolek (right), a species of shrike confined to west Africa.

Bourghou grassland has been replanted and new areas established which are beneficial both to resident and migratory birds.

Now, early in the third week of January with the dry-season well advanced, my journey into the delta is just beginning. Behind me, glinting in the light of late afternoon, lies the barrage across the Niger at Markala. A short distance ahead a fan of dirt tracks turns off the tar-sealed road and weaves through thick mixed scrub and dry woodland following the course of the river. It is best not to be driving on these deeply rutted and wild tracks after dark, so I follow the track for a few kilometres until the sun weakens behind a veil of dust and haze lying across the horizon. Then I stop and find a place to camp and after a cup of tea there is still light enough for a walk to see what is about.

In the evening stillness I can hear a few red-throated bee-eaters hawking insects overhead. The drone of a wasp or the whirring click of a flying beetle, then the snap of a bill closing quickly. A yellow wagtail is running and jumping at clouds of flying insects over a damp patch of grass in the river bed. Two wood sandpipers are feeding with some little-ringed plover at a pool in the sand banks further along the river. In the shallows are small parties of ruff, and by a pool under the far bank, three African spoonbills stand preening.

The next day I continue my journey. The only traffic on these tracks are occasional donkey carts trading between villages ferrying people and baggage. Sometimes mopeds pass, or there are lorries taking larger loads up into the delta, but for much of the day I seem to be the only vehicle on the road.

The long-tailed nightjar is common in the dryer parts of the flood plain. Their call is a wooden purring call that is held for a few seconds and ends in a short metallic gulp.

The village of Seri on the north-eastern side of the delta. The flood free areas of higher ground where the villages are are known locally as toguérés. Toguérés are Sahelian in character, dependent on the seasonal rains and are small in comparison to the extensive areas of floodplain, marsh and lakes. The general habitat is acacia woodlands and shrubby thickets interlaced by open grassy areas, with a few tamarind and fig trees.

Away from the bushes and thicker scrub along the river bank the landscape is dotted with termite mounds. Each species fashions its own distinctive type, adding a bizarre element to the dry and dusty scrub. Stalagmitic spikes and piles of ochre clay that the sun has fired to the hardness of earthenware; squat chimney pots with overhanging tops that are runnelled and pitted by seasonal winds and rain; then there are the mounds that raise enormous fluted turrets and cones high above the vegetation. This range of convenient tall perches, is great for rollers, shrikes and sometimes kestrels, but it is a landscape especially designed for wheatears.

On one large patch of ground, where the termitaria have been exposed by a grass fire, are two or three common wheatears. There's an Isabelline too, and on the other side a black-eared wheatear that appears to prefer the higher vantage of an acacia than that of the termite mounds.

Here in the Sahel, a habitat used extensively by visiting wheatears, the daytime temperature at ground level frequently reaches 40°C or more. But only a little way above the surface it can be 2° or 3°C cooler. It is not surprising that wheatears will take every opportunity to perch on even the slightest elevation. It also gives them a better vantage point from which to search for food, but it helps a little to keep them a fraction cooler as well.

In a while I stop to watch another wheatear, but this one is different; it is noticeably larger and slightly longer winged than many I have been seeing

WHITE STORKS

A small flock of white storks descending into an area of termitaria grassland in the delta. Since the early 1960s the number of white storks returning each year to breed in Europe has been steadily decreasing. The main factors causing the long-term decline can be found in Africa.

White storks from west of their migratory divide in Europe winter in West Africa, frequenting most often the dry steppes of the Sahel and Sudan Savanna. They visit wetlands and cultivation too, wandering about on the ground searching for local abundances of food. Before the cycle of drought years began plagues of migrating locusts frequently swarmed in the main wintering areas of the storks and were important prey for them. But drought killed the locust and since the late 1940s locust invasions have been controlled with insecticides whenever possible. Deprived of an important source of food and exposed to toxic chemicals, as well as facing habitat degredation because of drought and 'desertification' has led to their reduced numbers. After 'bad' winters in Africa, white storks arrive later on the breeding grounds and are less successful in raising young.

Hunting is another problem white storks face in Africa. Because of the shortfall in their normal food supply, they forage more often in populated areas exposing themselves to danger. To a villager without adequate nourishment but with a spear or bow and arrow, or perhaps one expensive cartridge for an ancient gun, a white stork foraging on the ground presents a relatively easy and 'cost effective' target.

Not long ago during the spring migration over Eilat in Israel, among a flock of white storks spiralling against the blue sky, one bird was seen with a spear protruding from its side.

over the past few days and is much richer and darker coloured on the undersides. I am sure it is a Greenland wheatear. Standing alert in the lattice of sharp-edged shadows under a small bush it watches the ground beyond the spread of shade, its bill held half open as if panting. Suddenly it dashes out into the heat and bright sunlight to snatch something small that has tumbled into the hollow of a sunbaked hoof print. Then just as quickly it returns

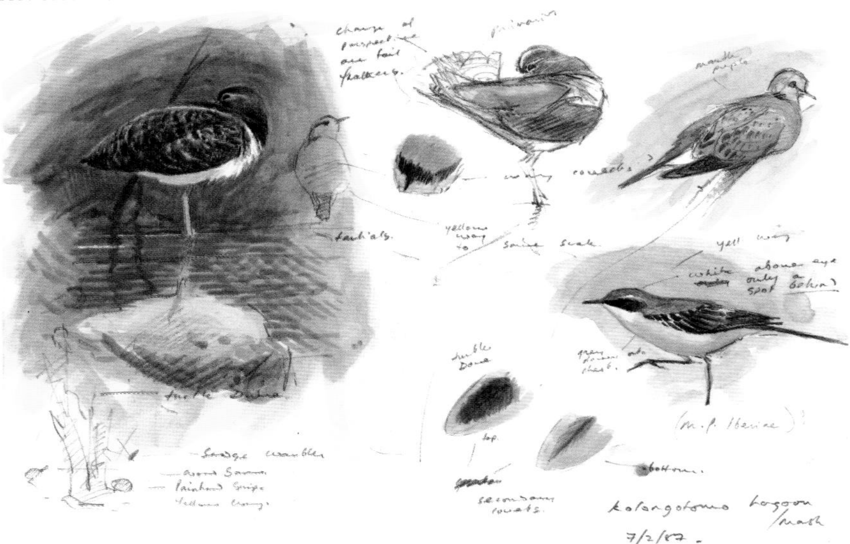

Studies of turtle doves, yellow wagtail and painted snipe. The snipe are strikingly patterned and extremely beautiful waders that are found across the Orient and Australasia as well as Africa. Painted snipe are most active at twilight and sometimes at night. By day they roost, quite often communally, in dense wetland vegetation.

to the shade and stands panting again. This is not the only migrant I have seen coping with the heat either by quickly seeking shade or panting. Generally, most migrant visitors to Africa will experience much higher mean daytime temperatures than they experienced in their summer home. For a Greenland wheatear the difference is considerable, but might not necessarily be a disadvantage. Higher average temperature generally lessens the overall maintenance needs for birds; they need to use less of their energy in keeping warm. As well as the days being far hotter, the nights in Africa are warmer and they are longer too. Other aspects of the birds' lives change in the tropics. They do not have the additional stress of breeding, which in the summer meant having to find extra food for hungry young. All these aspects combine to reduce the overall metabolic demands that migrant birds make on the African ecosystem to about 60% of their total requirements during the northern temperate summer. But life for migrants in Africa is not easy. They will have to defend feeding territories, learn about their new environment, avoid predators, and in some places face the consequences of habitat degradation or loss.

Soon the dirt track reaches a backwater of the river again and follows the high flood bank beside it; on one side of the road the milky green waters slide gently between lush green banks. Stretching away into the haze on the other side is a mosaic of small dykes and channels dividing a huge spread of rice fields.

In the sunken parcels of land are sacks of grain ready for collecting, and there are loose piles and ricks of rice stalks and husks. From the pile tops crested larks are singing and one provides a good field of view for an Abyssinian roller. In the litter of stalks on the ground a bluethroat is foraging.

In some of the fields small groups of villagers, mostly women, are winnowing and gleaning by hand. In other fields teams of men and boys work bullocks pulling ploughs. The air above them is filled with raptors – two or

Winnowing rice.

Sketches of marsh harrier, black-shouldered kite, spur-winged plover, great snipe, and a tail-less yellow wagtail. Between January and late March or early April, the yellow wagtail undergoes a pre-breeding partial moult replacing the body feathers, the tertials, some of the wing coverts, and many or all of the tail feathers. However, by the time the northward migration is due, it will be brightly and fully feathered again.

three marsh harriers, black-shouldered kites, a few Montagu's harriers, and a Lanner falcon flying fast overhead.

There are also very large numbers of pigeons and doves, a lot of them mourning and African collared doves and a few speckled pigeons. But they are greatly outnumbered by absolutely thousands of turtle doves, all of them travellers from north of the Sahara and one of the few seed-eating long-distance migrants.

On arrival in sub-Saharan Africa turtle doves pass through the Sahel and travel on into the Sudan Savanna and Guinea Savanna edges where the rains have already produced both a wild and a cultivated seed crop, so there is a food supply available immediately. Then, from January and February onwards, they return north and the numbers in the Sahel begin to build up, particularly in the inundation zone, where the rice harvest and naturally seeding grasses after the retreat of the flood produce an abundance of food. There is estimated to be over 700,000 turtle doves in the delta at their peak.

Walking out along the network of paths on top of the dykes, which ring each field like the dry crust around a pie dish, I push a male yellow wagtail into the open from the shadow of a bush in the ditch. As I walk along the bird keeps low down weaving in and out of the clots of vegetation and muddy margins at the bottom. As it crosses an open patch of ground I can see why it seems reluctant to fly – it is moulting and has no tail at all.

Trapped behind a small weir and between two raised tracks at the far end of the village of Kolongotomo is a triangle of watery habitat about the size of a large suburban garden. In one corner is a tangled thicket of drowned acacia with birds in abundance, so finding a shady spot beneath a flowering acacia on the bank, I settle to watch what is happening.

Swallow-tailed kites, a resident species, and sedge warblers. As they are very active and noisy, sedge warblers are one of the most conspicuous small migrants in the delta.

Dragonflies dart in and out of the flickering sunlight and lacework of dark shadows under the dome of thorns, and lizards scurry after flies along the bark.

Sedge warblers are busy everywhere, calling frequently as they weave through the strips of sunlight busily picking insects as they go. Further down towards the shallow end of the lagoon, two wood sandpipers work their way along the sticky mud edge. Suddenly there is a whirring flash of brick red and brilliant blue, and in a second a malachite kingfisher is bobbing its head and swaying on a overhanging branch close by – after a brief pause and a bob or two more, it is gone.

In the sunlight there are yellow wagtails strutting about and fluttering lightly across the vegetation in the water, snatching insects as they go. In the damp margins further down towards the weir common snipe show themselves, feeding in close company with jacanas and a single black crake. It is a striking mix of birds from 'home' that I know well and species much less familiar. Then creeping into view comes one of the most astonishing sightings I have had so far in Africa. It is a migrant that I never thought I would find again on my journey. Skulking through the thick mats of aquatic vegetation is a spotted crake.

It is about five months ago during the southward migration season that I glimpsed that spotted crake creeping across the patch of mud on the damp autumn fens of East Anglia. Of course this is not the same bird, but in between then and now I have seen no other. So in my mind's eye the sudden appearance of this bird in tropical West Africa directly links seasons that are worlds apart. In making the journey this spotted crake will have mostly roosted by day and flown by night, keeping low down as it flew, sometimes just a few metres above the ground. Some or its kind will have ended their migration at a wetland in southern Europe or North Africa, but many more will have travelled on across the Sahara to find a winter home among dense

A fig tree in the 'transition zone' near Youvarou. In some areas the transition from flood-free to regularly flooded land is sudden, in other places, where the flood has not reached for years, the change is gradual and the zone very wide.

vegetation in a quiet waterway somewhere in Africa – somewhere just like this.

It is now mid-morning on a day at the very end of January and I have reached the edge of the retreating flood. The inundated wetlands of the floodplain are dominated by perennial grassland of mostly wild rice and bourghou grass. Ahead, as far as the eye can see, is an ochre sea of trampled bourghou that in the distance changes colour to a lusher green. The line marks the limit of the grass still afloat on the receding flood.

This is cattle country – huge herds are spread out 'wall to wall' like a slowly moving patchwork laid from shimmering horizon to horizon. Four or five hundred, perhaps even thousands of cattle are in view, but I can only guess. Swirling, darting and fluttering in and out of each herd are swarms of cattle egrets, and everywhere there are clouds of yellow wagtails. Above them common pratincoles, with their graceful tern-like flight, sweep backwards and forwards; all of the birds are feeding on insects disturbed by the trampling cattle. There are many sedge warblers in the grass as well, a number of whinchats, a flock of lesser kestrels milling about overhead, and in the distance a small party of white storks on the ground. But downwind of one cattle herd are an enormous number of sand martins swirling about in the rising plume of disturbed insects. Gatherings like this, where migrants

A marsh harrier glides over a small flock of gargeney at a lagoon close to Mopti, the commercial heart of the delta.

greatly outnumber residents, occur quite often where an abundant food supply is available. It is an incredible sight.

In the warm dusty breeze blowing across the floodplain there are a number of harriers; three or four marsh harriers, a 'ringtail' and an adult male Montagu's drifting into the wind low down over the bourghou. Every so often one of them checks its flight, veering suddenly and flicking itself down in a flash when a possible meal is surprised in the rustling grass.

Montagu's harriers passing cattle assembled around the village of Ndobe, a toguéré far out on the floodplain.

At these latitudes twilight is brief. The sun drops quickly through the dust layers on the horizon and the wind drops and it soon turns cold under clear skies and a bright canopy of stars. In the darkness, with a small fire burning, I listen to the sound of cicadas, frogs or crying plovers, and write my notes by lamplight. One night I am disturbed by the rumble of cattle being moved to fresh pastures, the whistling and hollering herdsmen flashing torch-lights that flicker through the dust like lightening in a storm cloud.

At last I have now reached the flood. For the last stage of this journey, I must try and find a pirogue to hire and someone to pole me through the marsh and mass of channels to Lake Debo which lies at the centre of the delta. It takes a while to find transport, but in a day I am on my way.

A fish eagle is circling above the camp as we leave, drifting on broad dark wings it calls – that magical sound of Africa again. A handful of sand martins weave about in the warm breeze above the river bank, and with them are a few African sand martins. They differ from the Palearctic birds in being fractionally smaller, but more obviously they lack the chest-band, instead the whole throat and chest area are a greyish mouse brown.

All along the waterways there are fishermen tending lines and nets from the bank, or from pirogues pushed to rest into the bourghou. On low mud banks lines of long-tailed cormorants rest and preen. Black-winged stilts, small flocks of black-tailed godwits and sacred ibis come and go. Everywhere there are hordes of yellow wagtails and an abundance of marsh harriers. Whiskered, gull-billed and white-winged black terns drift overhead.

Now, much closer to open water, the channels have grown wider and the waters slowed and cleared. The number of birds all around has been growing steadily, then in the distance a distinct rough croaking roar begins to rise above the calls of passing terns and rustling wind in the sea of floating grass. With more and more birds on the move all around, Tielde cannot be far away now. In a while the pirogue slides into open water, and there, stretched across the middle-distance, is perhaps the most spectacular concentration of human and bird-life in Africa. The sight is stunning.

Studies of Temminck's stint and ruff. From December to February there are almost 200,000 ruff in the Inundation Zone and in many Sahelian wetlands they outnumber all other waders put together.

Tielde is a seasonal fishing camp built as soon as the flood waters subside enough to expose a faint rise in the mud on the western edge of Lake Debo. Past the camp runs a shallow channel that squeezes the falling flood-waters as they escape from the basin of the delta into the lake. Moving with the water are teeming multitudes of fish that spawned with the rising flood and now must escape its progressive drying out. It is to harvest this huge seasonal abundance that the camp is built each year alongside the only escape route for the fish. Above the camp drifts a permanent haze of wood-smoke as the huge daily fish catch is processed, dried and cured. Piles of dried fish lie in front of every hut where people are busy weighing, sorting, smoking and drying fish of many different kinds – baskets of shiny brown strips, crisp orange rings curled like doughnuts, larger fillets spiked on sticks, smouldering fires and small mud-brick kilns, the ground in between carpeted with shiny fish scales that sparkle in the harsh sunlight.

Sharing the Tielde's seasonal abundance of fish is a thronging multitude of birds; in the near vicinity of the camp there must be many, many thousands; little and yellow-billed egrets, black and great white herons and long-tailed cormorants. Every available perch along the dams has an egret, a heron or a pied kingfisher perched there. Above all of this is a mass of terns and gulls; white-winged black, whiskered, gull-billed and Caspian terns; grey-headed gulls, and on quieter stretches of water away from the dams are a few lesser black-backed gulls.

Just beyond the camp are flocks of glossy ibis, rafts of pintail and garganey, passing streams of white-faced whistling ducks, and knob-billed geese. Waders too are here in large numbers. Kittlitz's sandplovers, black-tailed godwits, wood and curlew sandpipers, greenshank, redshank, curlew, little stints, ringed plover and huge numbers of ruff.

By far the largest numbers of birds that have congregated here are migrants from Eurasia, just as at virtually every other Afro-tropical wetland at this time of year. During the winter of 1986–87 less than 5% of the total

One of the five fish dams at Tielde on the edge of Lake Debo. At its busiest, Tielde has almost two thousand people living in a close assembly of straw and grass huts divided by 'corridors' and 'streets' screened with mats of grass and reed. Day or night, activity never ceases; they have only six weeks to cash in on the abundance.

number of wildfowl in the inland delta in Mali were Afro-tropical species, and most of those were local white-faced whistling duck. The fact that so many migrants can claim these wetlands almost as their own is mainly because resident species belonging to the Anatidae – ducks, geese and swans – belong to different genera from the visiting Palearctic species. The ecological niches that the resident species fill differ from those sought by the multitude of incoming migrants. The residents are dependent on the Sahelian wetlands throughout their annual cycle but the sudden increase in available food, brought on by the floods, cannot be fully exploited by them alone as their population is adjusted to the period when food is scarcest. A similar ecological situation occurs for waders where there are many fewer resident African species of the Scolopacidae – the family that includes among others godwits, sandpipers, snipe, stints and ruff.

Seeing the huge numbers of birds catching fish around the dams at Tielde, I wonder what impact they have on the fish resources of the lakes, and whether there is resentment from people who generally have little to maintain themselves on through the whole year, so need to store a seasonal abundance? Are the birds thought to be 'stealing' the fish? Here in Mali the attitude of the fishing people seems to be that when they could see plenty of birds, then there must be plenty of fish which is a good sign for them; if there were not the birds, there would not be fish. There seems to be some realisation that they are equally dependent on the same resource. The only exception is the threat from pelicans that can clear out a pool system in hours. A few years ago the fishermen wanted to shoot the whole lot, although they risked a fine, but the IUCN persuaded them that it was not the best solution to the problem. Instead it was suggested that they station boys in boats to keep disturbing the pelicans preventing them from landing if they looked like threatening the fishing in a particular area.

At dusk, as the light from lanterns and fires start to flicker through Tielde, I wind my way back to the hut I have been loaned for the few days that I am here. The night is busy with the scuttling and clicking of cockroaches, and the hubbub of village life that never stops and all the while coming through the darkness the sound of the birds by the dams. I wake early and see streams of pintail and garganey pouring overhead in the half-light before dawn, on the move between feeding and roosting sites. The whistling of wind in many thousands of wings clearly audible in the early morning stillness.

If there is one location I am reluctant leave on the whole migratory journey so far, then this is it. I have never been to a place so rich in experiences of people and birds. It is the way that they live their lives so closely together that has excited me; both almost totally dependant on the same life-giving flood. I could stay here painting and sketching for the rest of the season, but it is now 10th February and I am still over 4000km from my home in Europe. There, spring is not so very far away, so I must get a move on.

A host of Eurasian migrants at Lake Debo with a pirogue shimmering in the distance beyond them. The ducks are garganey and pintail, the two species of wildfowl that occur here in the largest numbers, to the point of outnumbering all other visiting and resident wildfowl put together.

CHAPTER TEN

African Landscapes

Keeping such a watchful eye on the birds and changing African landscape, it is impossible not to notice signs that tell of the fragility of these sub-Saharan lands. Now in mid-February I watch the Sudan Savanna of Burkina Faso and Niger slip by over a period of days. The dry-season is well advanced and the vegetation looks scorched and brittle. There are whirring flocks of firefinches and manikins and every few minutes the flash of white from the tail of a wheatear flitting from boulder to boulder along the roadside. Here and there are baobabs towering above the lower canopy of light thorn and scrub. Their limbs provide good vantage points for birds like black-eared wheatears, chanting goshawks, grey kestrels and a Bateleur eagle.

But I also notice bundles of wood piled by the roadside and every so often I have to pull over to make way for huge lorries laden down with timber. There are groups of boys with donkeys weighed down with sticks and logs. In most of the developing world people rely on wood and charcoal for cooking and heating. Wood forms 97% of Mali's total annual energy consumption, and in Burkina Faso it is 94%. Using wood as fuel not only means that larger and more mature trees are felled, but also the low, shrubby vegetation is cut as well. Trees around the major urban areas, where demand for fuel-wood is concentrated, have all but disappeared. In the rural areas, scrublands around villages are being cleared in ever widening circles. Faced with walking further and further in search of wood, or paying

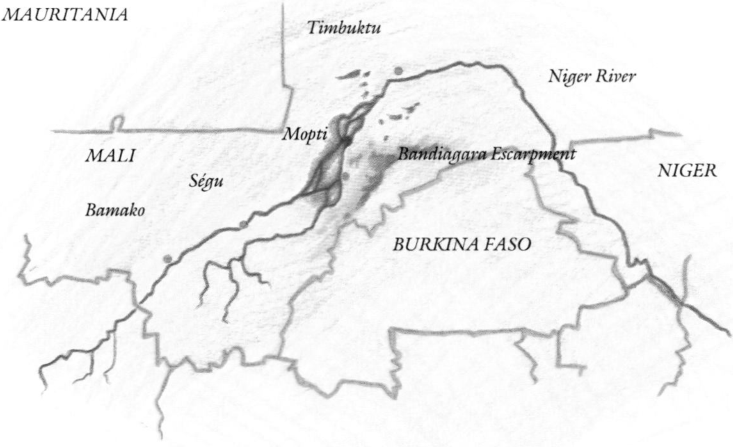

These two sketches sum up the kind of visual contrasts that, before making the journey with the migrants, I was anxious to capture but could not foresee. In the top sketch a male redstart approaches a nest hole in a pine tree in a forest north of the Arctic circle. The bottom sketch also shows a redstart, but at the opposite extreme of its annual cycle. It is occupying a similar habitat, typically where the ground is clear of dense undergrowth in the shelter of fairly open wooded country, but this time in the southern Sahara.

Sunlight and shadows in the Sahel.

a higher price for it, villagers have turned to burning more cattle dung, husks and other agricultural residues, some of which would have otherwise gone back on to the fields to enrich the soil. The removal of trees and scrub exposes the soil to erosion and it is lost forever.

As well as the loss of vegetation, there have been other long-term economic and social changes in land-use which has seen this fragile asset overcultivated and overgrazed. Poor irrigation and the prolonged drought over the past two decades have also taken their toll. Straining under these pressures the land has grown increasingly weak, becoming so degraded that over large areas it has lost its capacity to support cultivation and livestock grazing. When a crisis occurs, and it is usually drought that triggers such a crisis, no safety margin exists to cushion the environment. If the crisis lasts for more than a season or two, the land cannot recover quickly enough and it begins to 'die'. An ugly situation that has produced an ugly word – 'desertification'.

As well as the tragic human consequences of the deepening ecological crisis over much of Sahelian Africa, this catastrophe has had an enormous effect on the numbers of birds returning to Europe. After the major Sahelian drought of 1984, the number of sand martins returning to one colony in Scotland the following spring was less than a third of the numbers that departed the previous Autumn. A massive drop even after taking into account the numbers that usually perish on the journey to and from Africa. But bad drought years had begun to effect sand martins long before that. The British breeding population is now less than 10% of what it was 20 years ago.

Whitethroats and sedge warblers have been affected too. The British

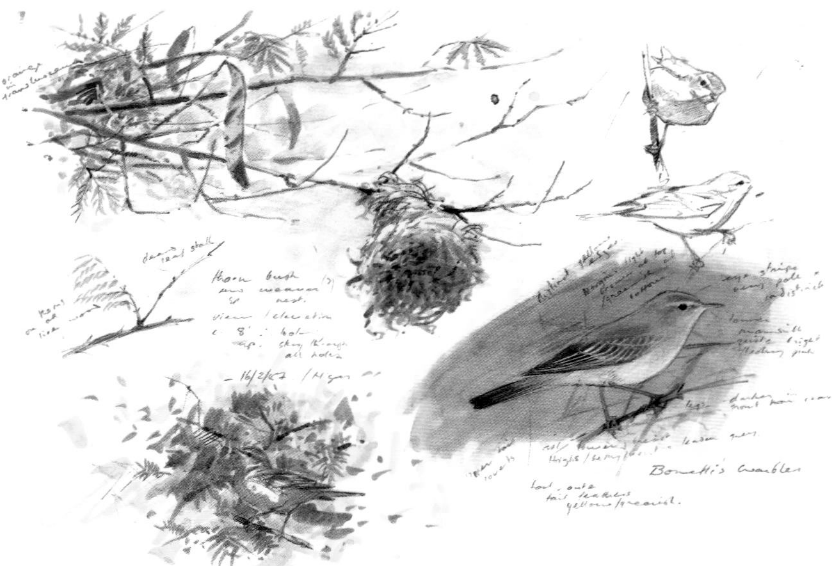

Sketches of acacia with seed pod, weaver nest and Bonelli's warbler. Closely related to the willow warbler, Bonelli's is very much a southern Europe replacement for it in summer. South of the Sahara Bonelli's warbler's winter distribution is along the northern edge of the willow warbler's.

population of whitethroats crashed in the winter of 1968–69 and although it managed to recover to a degree, it plummeted again after the 1984 Sahelian drought. The whitethroat population crash has quite a direct link with the Sahelian droughts. Like many other insectivorous warblers they fatten up on the berries of the saltbush *Salvadora persica* before leaving Africa. But the saltbush cannot withstand prolonged drought and has died out over large areas, effectively leaving the birds without the fuel to get them home.

With drought and desertification affecting the Sahel, pressure is building up on the Sudan and Guinea Savannas that lie further south. Many migrant birds utilise these two vegetation zones in winter. Increasing human pressure, and the changes in land-use that it encourages, will effect the habitats in which many of 'our' migrants spend the winter. Any change in their carrying capacity will affect migrant, as well as resident, birds.

After flowing through virtual desert over the 'Niger Bend', the Niger river changes its character. From Ansongo in Mali to Niamey in Niger it is more tightly confined by rocky escarpments and hurries along, around long ribbons of rock, smooth boulder outcrops and palm covered islands that twist and split the flow of water into swirling pools and channels. This stretch of the river running through the Sahel has a very different look and feel to it, so I will take a closer look.

It is now February the 19th. Walking on the east bank near Sonsoni-Haousa, a village 65 kilometres north of Niamey I watch an osprey circling high above the river in the early morning breeze, slowly making its way downstream. On the grassy river edges and around the trailing spits of gravel and sand among quieter waters are wagtails, mostly African pied, but there are a few yellow wagtails too. A silted meander has a small flock of

Cattle and a green sandpiper in a swampy area close to the town of Nalougou in Burkina Faso. Green sandpipers frequent freshwater streams, pools and river edges throughout sub-Saharan Africa during the winter.

ruff, there is a green sandpiper and Temminck's stint too, and one or two common sandpiper feeding.

The alluvial plain is covered in a mosaic of maize and sorghum spread among an orchard-like spacing of acacias, lime trees, and doum palm and by scrubby gulleys running down from the escarpment. Warblers are numerous here; most seem to be Bonelli's, but subalpine, with their noisy rattling churr, are conspicuous too. There are orphean warblers, chiffchaffs and, weaving through the spikes of grass tussocks on the rocky slopes of the escarpment, a party of resident cricket warblers. The others are migrants, but cricket warblers are small residents confined to scrubland along the southern edge of the Sahara. Not surprisingly there are wheatears here too, as there have been in virtually every location I have been to so far in West Africa. Then suddenly, from below a cluster of palms, flies a wryneck. They are uncommon or rare winter visitors to wooded grasslands, cultivation and plantations from Sénégal and Gambia eastwards to Ethiopia and Sudan. I have been lucky to see one.

Beside the river is a continuous strip of cultivated ground made up of individual garden-sized plots fenced by planted thorns, netting or wattles of palms to exclude wandering livestock. Inside are neatly spaced rows of aubergines and carrots, cabbages and peppers, lettuces and tomatoes. Spaced among them are clusters of mango trees.

By mid-morning I have started to be bothered by the flies. I also need

Booted eagle (top left), Montagu's harrier and long-legged buzzard (centre) at Dogondoutchi in Niger.

some fresh vegetables, so I sit for a while with a gardener discussing prices away from the flies in the cool shade of a mango. It is like being in a light and airy room. Thin bright slits of light pour in through a leafy ceiling and dapple the floor. All the while there is a continuous hum and buzzing noise; it is not an electric fan, but a mass of insects in the canopy which is attracting large numbers of sedge warblers.

The mango, like the oak in Europe, harbours a greater insect fauna than almost any other tree. Each tree seems to hold 5 or 10 birds, rattling and churring as they chase in and out of the leaves and flowering stems. In all the locations I have visited so far across West Africa I do not think I have yet come across a more confined concentration of small migrants in any one habitat. Like many other small migrants, these sedge warblers need to lay down large reserves of fat to fuel their journey home. To cross the Sahara from here they will need enough fuel for a flight of about 60 hours to reach their first refuelling stop in southern Europe. In six or seven weeks time the first sedge warblers will begin arriving in Europe. Although they are some time away from leaving here, perhaps these birds are busy defending rich feeding territories in that vital building-up period.

At this point of the dry-season, the Sahel is dotted with areas of water that are much smaller than the major rivers and their wetlands, but they are equally as important for migrants. They are relics of the rains, spring pools or small ponds trapped by local barrage systems near towns and villages, and range in size from puddles to lakes. On the outskirts of Dogondoutchi, a village 200 km east of Niamey, is a basin of mud and water the size of a small city park and I reach it early in the morning of February 21st. In the centre is standing water clogged with spreading patches of aquatic vegetation, its surface flecked with the milky white and soft violet of massed water lilies. The wind is scorching hot and, running through the surrounding scrub in twisting columns, pulls dust and straws into the air, rattles seeds and drags leaves along the ground and flips up the corners of lilly pads as it gusts across the water.

There are a number of resident birds; fulvous and white-faced whistling duck, sacred ibis, black-necked heron, African spoonbill and a host of pigeons, scrub-robins, camaropteras and sunbirds. But migrants outnumber them. There are scattered flocks of garganey, about 100–150 in all. There is also a handful of shoveler. I am surprised to see coot here, as only relatively few cross the Sahara, most of the migrant European populations reach western Europe and the Mediterranean basin, with a few reaching North Africa for the winter. A fisherman wading out to retrieve his catch pushes an even scarcer Palearctic visitor into view from the cover of vegetation at the water's edge – a ferruginous duck. They migrate from the steppes of Eastern Europe and beyond and only small numbers, counted in hundreds, reach the northern savannas of West Africa and in some years they are totally absent.

Even with only a thin vegetated margin there are still good numbers of purple herons here, they usually favour dense aquatic vegetation; in the Niger delta I had seen hundreds. What vegetation there is beside the water has marsh harriers drifting over it; above them in the increasing heat and blustery wind of late-morning other raptors are moving. A long-legged buzzard circles high above and stacked on other thermals are two booted and a Whalberg's eagle, with a few black kites lower down. There is a confusion of yellow wagtail races around the waters edge and among the livestock brought down to drink. In the winter quarters they are closely associated with grazing herbivores, both wild and domestic, a niche that is little exploited by any small African birds. One tribal name for the yellow wagtail is kadima mbuzi – the goat herd.

The area also provides rich pickings for migrant waders. Numerous birds

An immature male Montagu's harrier (top left), sacred ibis and Temminck's stint (bottom row). Montagu's harrier ranges over all kinds of open country in Africa, but seems to be attracted to wetland margins with low surrounding vegetation.

Different species and races of wheatears sketched for plumage detail only. Whenever the opportunity arose on the journey across West Africa, the Sahara and the Maghreb, one more 'feather map' was added to the sequence. The flashing white rump and varying amounts of black and white patterning on the tail is the most striking characteristic of most wheatear species in flight, including isabelline, desert, black-eared, mourning, white crowned black and nominate wheatear, all of which are shown here. The only one illustrated which does not is the red-rumped.

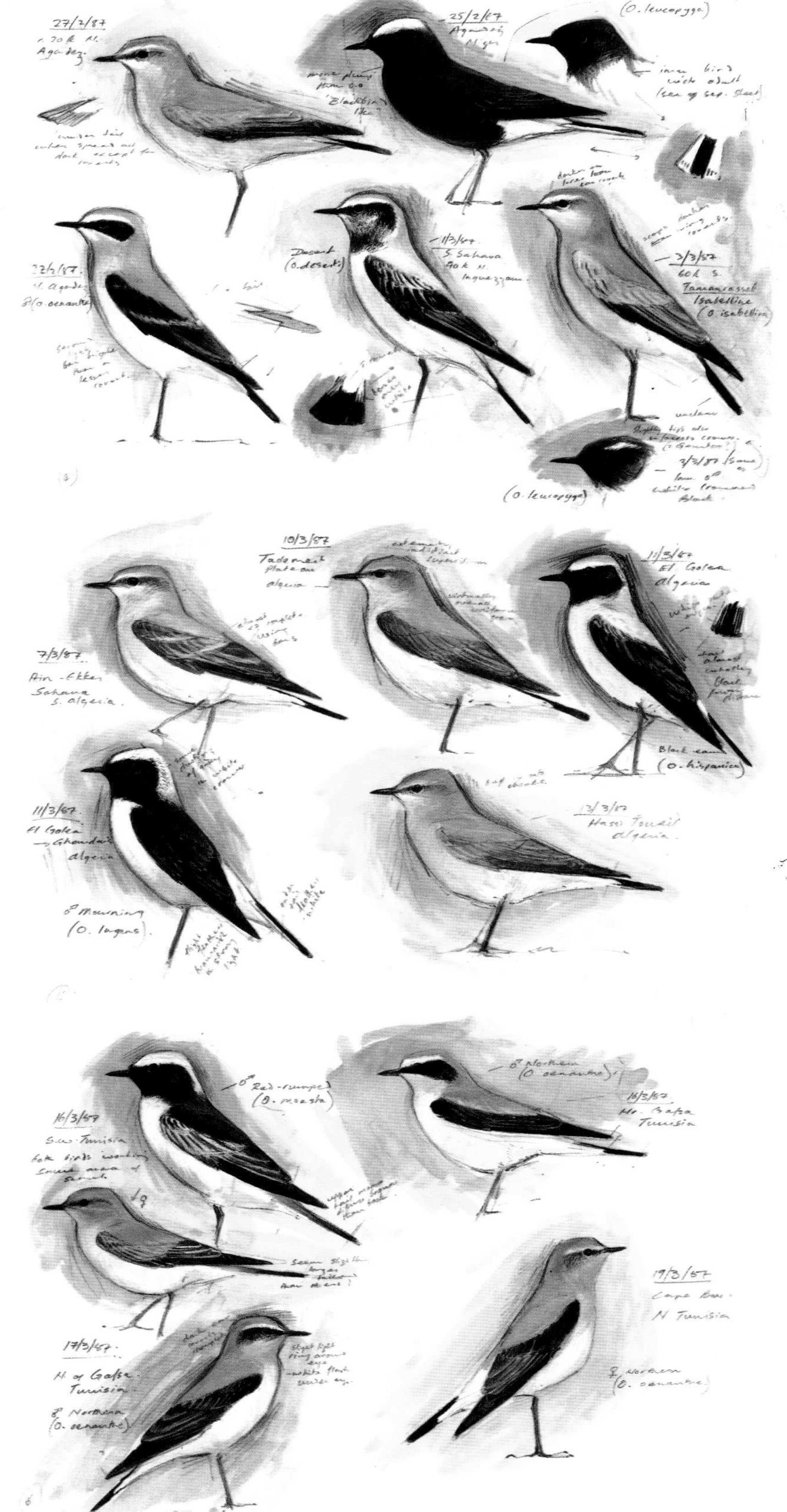
27/2/87
Agadez
(O. leucopyga)
25/2/87
Niger
"Blackbird like"
Desert
(O. deserti)
1/3/87
S. Sahara
3/3/87
60k S.
Tamanrasset
Isabelline
(O. isabellina)
(O. leucopyga)
10/3/87
Tademait
Plateau
Algeria
11/3/87
El Golea
Algeria
7/3/87
Ain-Ekker
Sahara
S. Algeria
Black-eared
(O. hispanica)
11/3/87
El Golea
Algeria
♂ Mourning
(O. lugens)
13/3/87
Algeria
♂ Red-rumped
(O. moesta)
16/3/87
Tunisia
♂ Northern
(O. oenanthe)
16/3/87
Tunisia
17/3/87
Tunisia
♀ Northern
(O. oenanthe)
19/3/87
N Tunisia
♀ Northern
(O. oenanthe)

are feeding all along the muddy shallows; green and wood sandpipers, little ringed plovers, common snipe, black-winged stilts and in one corner a flock of about 150 ruff. There are a few avocets as well, a species which is a fairly common visitor to sub-Saharan wetlands of the northern tropics like this. Here and there in the dappled shade under partly submerged and drowned acacias a few Temminck's stints are feeding. There are some little stints picking busily at the surface, and a flock 10 greenshanks in the shadow of an overhanging thorn tree. There are marsh and curlew sandpipers, and a few spotted redshanks to complete the picture. The thorn thickets and bushes at the wetland edge are thick with warblers; sedge and subalpine, olivaceous and Bonelli's, chiffchaffs and whitethroats.

Without any scientific evidence, I am sure that the migrant birds here at Dogondoutchi outnumber resident African species by at least ten to one. It is clear even to the casual observer that it is not only the large wetlands and river systems that are vital to the migratory strategy of migrants. Even the smallest areas of water are crucial, particularly at this time of year prior to their journey home. Within sight of the desert, sites like this offer the last opportunity to feed and refuel. A migrant can go no further without actually starting the journey out of Africa. Although there are still a few weeks to go before the largest numbers depart, some will already be on their way. There is a great sense of preparation in those that are here as they get ready to change seasons.

Agadez is a small town in northern Niger lying by a broad sand river in the marchlands of the great Sahara desert. For centuries the economic and political power of the Taureg people of this region was derived from its place on the ancient trans-Saharan caravan routes. Now a tar-sealed road runs north for 250 kilometres from Agadez to Arlit, but from there north the road ends, disintegrating rapidly into a wild trail of hard tracks and pistes that for a further 2000 kilometres wind their way across the Sahara.

It is now March 1st and in the sharp cold air of early morning I am heading north on the road out of Arlit across an open rolling plain of grit and sand. Tilted ridges and piles of rock lie like enormous handfuls of loose change strewn on a table. Growing in isolated tufts are short bushy herbs and grasses dried and made brittle by the scorching winds. The blue, sharp toothed and ragged outline of the Aïr mountains lie all along the distant eastern horizon.

The passage of the vehicle along the road disturbs a short-toed eagle that flies low from one large boulder pile, gaining little height in the coolness of early morning, before slipping out of sight. Wheatears flit from boulder to boulder; one of them is an Isabelline. They are slightly larger and longer-legged, and look more robust than the Eurasian wheatear, and migrate to Africa from breeding grounds on the dry steppes and semi-desert, from Anatolia eastwards across central Asia to Manchuria.

The move from northern Sahel to sub-desert is not abrupt; it appears to be nothing more than a gradual transition from a parched to an extremely parched landscape. The few thorn trees and stands of *Calotropis*, a strange lush-looking plant, that is unpalatable to humans and livestock and of little

Studies of adult and immature white-crowned black wheatear. A true Saharan species characteristic of inhospitable desert regions, but locally it also becomes a bird of habitation and oases.

attraction to birds, stand isolated among the thin-bladed grassy tussocks. Birds are perhaps the best indicators of the habitat type; still there are white-fronted finch larks and bar-tailed desert larks foraging in the long morning shadows. Then for the first time I see a hoopoe lark, one of the largest and most beautiful larks, a species characteristic of the sub-Saharan and North African desert fringes.

By lunchtime I have reached a track that runs off from the road near the ouadi Tamazelak. It threads around boulder piles and sandy hollows for five kilometres to an indistinct outcrop of rock. The rounded slabs are burnt a deep ochre and stacked to the height of a two-storey house and around its base is a cluster of thorn scrub and grass. On one large slab near the top is carved the beautifully simple shape of a giraffe, the tilt of the rock across the morning light outlining the animal's form and patterned coat in shadow. In hollows, under overhangs, and on sheltered surfaces lower down there are other animals scratched in simple outline; running gazelles, wild goats and more giraffe; some of them animals not seen around here for perhaps a thousand years. This is art from the Neolithic age, graphic evidence that the Sahara has had a much greener past.

The road north begins to dip and climb slowly over low rolling stone hills

As little as 8–10,000 years ago, after the retreat of the last Eurasian ice-sheet, the ecological picture of Africa differed greatly from that of the present day.

Lying north-west of Timbuktu, in what is now desert, was the huge inland lake of Arouane, and further east was Megachad, a vast inland sea four times larger than the present Lake Chad. Mediterranean type vegetation spread south over the Sahara as far as the Tibesti and Aïr mountains where characteristically temperate tree species such as lime, ash and walnut flourished. To the south of the ancient lakes and inland seas, scrub and dry woodland and species of plant characteristic of tropical Africa spread north into the Sahara. Grazing animals and their predators followed; the white rhinoceros reached as far as the Ahaggar massif, and across the lush Saharan plains and light woodlands roamed herds of zebras, gazelles, elephant, lions and leopards.

Hunter-gatherers also roamed in this wilderness taking shelter in rock caves, where they left behind graphic evidence of the once green Sahara.

The earliest depictions are about 6000 year old and show the simple outlines of wild animals and their hunters. About a thousand years later domestic animals appear for the first time, at first only goats and sheep, then cattle are seen in ones and twos, marked on the cave walls by a more sophisticated hand.

Over time the depictions slowly change to show larger herds of livestock as early nomadic pastoralists moved more widely over the Sahara with larger and larger herds, creating an early civilisation whose economy was almost entirely dependant on cattle. But by this time, a long term climatic shift to dryer conditions had begun to see the Mediterranean species of tree replaced by those more typical of Sahelian vegetation and better able to take advantage of the dryer conditions. The meteorological background and causes of the climatic change remain unclear, but as temperatures rose and rainfall diminished, the vegetation entered a critical stage at the same time as it was under grazing pressure.

The cumulative effect was the gradual disintegration of the once green Sahara.

As well as the cave paintings, there are other relics of greener times. High up in the Tassili and Ahaggar mountains, sheltering in deep gulleys and clustered around gueltas or rock pools are ancient oleanders, olive and cypress trees, cut-off thousands of years ago from Mediterranean origins a thousand kilometres away.

In the remotest rock pools the strangest relics of wetter times survived. In 1876 a German explorer and trained naturalist recorded evidence of crocodiles in the Adrar N' Iforas massif. Their existence was doubted by some until a specimen was shot by a French Army captain in 1908.

The progression of changes in the Sahara will have effected migrants too. With a much more hospitable vegetation, the Sahara would have been a winter home to many, and those that had to cross it would have perhaps been able to stop and feed along the way. The present strategy of laying down large fat reserves to fuel the desert crossing could well have developed in birds only in the past few thousand years.

A male wheater about to begin its journey out of Africa. The timing of a migrants departure is correlated generally to the latitude in which it breeds; birds with a breeding destination in Spain can set off from Africa before birds that will end their journey in northern Scandinavia. If northern breeding birds arrived early their food supply might not be available in sufficient amounts and they would risk starvation.

criss-crossed by shallow gulleys. In some of them is scattered vegetation; compact thorn bushes and herb scrub which is used by desert nomads for fodder and fuel. There are spiky grasses and cram-cram, which has vicious barbed seed heads that cling to skin and clothing with the ferocity of tiny bundles of fish hooks.

In one gulley a flock of sheep and goats, and a few camels are browsing, 'watched' by a herdsman asleep on his camel. Not far ahead of them on the ground is a large group of white storks spread out feeding. Then, disturbed by the gradually approaching animals, they lift off, climbing quickly above the plains. There are 26 of them, and I watch as they circle tightly, rising rapidly in the hot updraughts. Soon they are lost against the intense brightness of the sky.

There are wheatears on the move too, and then suddenly swinging over a rocky bluff, the superb aerial elegance of a passing male pallid harrier flying low over the ground, lightly buoyant like a broad light grey leaf blowing in the wind.

The increasing heat of afternoon brings stronger winds from the north-east and four or five times each hour other migrants pass. There are sand martins on the move in ones and twos, flying differently to the lazy swinging back and forth across the breeze that I had watched so frequently on the floodplain in Mali. They seem to have a distinct purpose and direction. With the first arrivals of sand martins in Britain being before the end of March, and even earlier in southern Europe, these passing birds are on time.

Travelling through West Africa I have been paying the landscapes as much attention as the birds so as to try and get to grips with the different habitats that are so important for wintering migrants. Each habitat type has had a different and very striking ornithological image which to my eye has defined their differences and the changes between them. In front of me now is an image that confirms my move from semi-arid or sub-desert to the barren and hostile enormity of true desert.

The only standing features, and almost the only vegetation in the landscape, are the stunted shapes of a few thorn trees shrouded by thin veils of sand and dust that the wind is lifting. Pointing into wind under each tree are short streaks of dark shadow, and downwind on the other side lie hot patches of sun-scorched sand. Under one tree I make out the shape of a wheatear. It is crouching on the hot sunlit side where it is sheltered by the trunk from the wind and flying sand, but still exposed to the intense desert heat. I sit and watch it for a while, and in time see it change position, moving around the trunk to crouch in the shadow where, it is exposed to the stinging grittiness of the wind. It seems as if the wheatear on this occasion has actively sought the advantage of shade over that of shelter. Small pegs in the ground marking oil sites in the Libyan desert have been seen with semi-circles of foot marks around their base where small birds seeking shade have marked their movements in dodging the sun with the precision of a sundial. Perhaps this wheatear is physiologically primed for the long migration 'home' and tonight it will depart. If not tonight, then surely very soon for already the first birds are arriving in southern Britain. But whenever it leaves the first part of its journey north must be across 2000 kilometres of some of the most inhospitable land in the world – the Sahara desert.

CHAPTER ELEVEN

The Return

The Sahara is a desert of startling natural extravagance and extremes. Intense heat by day, from a sky that can be cloudless for half a year, gives way to bitter cold by night. What little rain there is falls violently in sudden showers, sometimes years apart. There is no overlay of soil, no vegetation or the scars of human workings to cover and hide the evidence of the geological past. Ancient granites, larvas and sandstones, and the many millenia of changes they have undergone, are laid out and exposed to the intense desert heat.

The Sahara, its name derived from an Arabic word meaning empty, is a desert three times larger than any other in the world. It covers over nine million square kilometres and stretches across Africa from the Atlantic coast in the west to the Red Sea in the east. It has no precise boundaries, ranging in width from 1500 to 2500 kilometres, the variation gauged by the erratic limits of wind-blown sand and by the irregular movement of a line on a seasonal rainfall map. It is a wilderness that is virtually uninhabitable to any living animal or plant without a special adaptation and most of it can offer virtually nothing to migrant birds. With practically no food, no water, no shade, and certainly no chance of turning back, it is a formidable and hostile ecological barrier.

The return spring migration begins in February and by late April is virtually complete, but this is the period when the dry-season in the northern Sahel is at its most intense. Trees are leafless and the ground is bare, effectively increasing the width of the desert itself to include much of the northern Sahel. Birds therefore must take-off further south than the limits of the desert proper. There are dangers in dust and sand storms. A disorientated bird could be forced to the ground, where it would be buffeted by the wind, or, taking time to seek shelter in a severe storm, would use up vital energy reserves, or even be buried by sand. A quick un-broken crossing increases the chances of survival.

However, there are some sectors of the desert that are less hostile to passage migrants. In the west, running parallel to the Atlantic coast from the Cayor Coastlands of Sénégal to Morocco, is a strip of desert a few hundred kilometres wide where there is dense scrub and scattered *acacias* maintained mostly by dewfall. There is some relief too in the mountain ranges that cover a quarter of the total desert area; the Ahaggar and Tassili N' Ajjer in the centre with the Adrar N' Iforas to the south, and the Aïr and Tibesti mountains in the east. Around rock pools, or gueltas, in the valleys and

Bruce Pearson

gulleys there is some vegetation and shelter to be had from the wind and sun.

The remaining desert area, and by far the largest, is a scorching wilderness of ergs and hamadas. Ergs are the classic rolling seas of sand; hamadas are plains of gravel strewn with coarse stones and rocks which spill out from the mountain ranges on an oceanic scale. It is the wind more than anything that you notice in the desert landscape. Even the slightest breeze brings up a fine dust from the ground. Long wisps and swirling powdery trails race across the sand, then vanish in seconds. As the day heats up the wind gains strength and becomes more turbulent, sometimes bringing with it a sand storm that in minutes creates a dark and dangerous twilight of ochre-yellow.

The illusion created by the enormity of this desert landscape is of an ocean with rocky islands and peninsulas jutting out from gulfs of wind rippled sand. One desert island is Garra Ekkar, on the border of Algeria and Niger. It is a silent lonely place that has the feel of some strange island city abandoned in the distant past to be slowly drowned by sand. Rock columns and eroded domes rise to the height of office blocks, their stonework faces cracked and split and coated in a flaking sheen of dark patina. The spaces between the rock columns are as wide as streets and blocked by centuries of wind blown sand. There are open spaces the size of city parks or plazas and these are littered with desert melons and a few small thorn trees. Suddenly there is sign of life in the corner of a park as a subalpine warbler begins to chatter. A desert wheatear appears soon after on some boulders at the far end. It is possible that they both will have wintered here.

As evening falls an Egyptian Vulture drifts along the skyline of towering stone blocks searching the 'streets' and gulleys below. In Garra Ekkar the shadows fall early and the temperature drops quickly. In the crisp cold air soon after dark the stars shine as bright as distant street lights and a lantern moon glows above.

My journey north across the desert is a little ahead of the main flood of migrants, but on a night like this it is worth getting comfortable and watching the face of the moon through the telescope. Moon-watching is a technique that can provide useful migration information. High flying nocturnal migrants will most likely pass undetected, but larger birds can be visible during the second or two it takes for them to pass across the moon's disc.

In the first hour I see no movement at all, but about twenty minutes after that a very small grainy cluster passes across the disc. Specific identification is impossible of course, but no matter, whatever their heading it was more or less northerly and in seeing them I feel I have glimpsed for a second an aspect of migration normally hidden from view.

For many years it was thought that oases would be particularly attractive to migrants on their journey across the desert, presenting the chance to feed and rest or shelter from adverse conditions among welcome greenery before continuing the journey. But, against the scale of the Sahara desert oases are extremely small, very remote and insignificantly few in number. It has been calculated that in over 500,000 square kilometres of desert east of the

Desert routes are marked all along the way by debris and litter. Burnt-out and abandoned cars sometimes offer shade to exhausted migrants. Many species have been recorded sheltering in such junk, from short-eared owls to little egrets.

Tibesti mountains, the total area covered by oases is less than 600 square kilometres so only a few of the many passing millions would find any reliable feeding opportunities. From recent evidence gathered by mist-netting and ringing birds at oases, it is now clear that they do play an important part in migration across the Sahara. Large numbers of birds land, mainly to rest, but also to refuel. It appears that most birds only stop at smaller oases for about a day, but might stop at larger oases for longer; pauses of 5 days, even three weeks, have been recorded. The length of stay also varies within a species. The lightest garden warblers (ie. those that have used up more of their fuel) stay the longest and feed actively throughout the day to replenish their reserves as quickly as possible; the heavier birds remain completely inactive and inconspicuous before leaving the same day after a short rest. The speed and direction of winds over the Sahara are of great importance to migrant birds crossing the desert; they determine the duration and influence the direction of the flight. Tail winds are particularly important if the desert crossing is to be non-stop. As a bird prepares to launch itself on the crossing it cannot predict the conditions that might prevail if it were to delay the journey by a few hours or even a few days in anticipation of more favourable conditions. The ecological state of the southern edge of the Sahara in spring does not favour birds that linger.

Tamanrasset is not a classic Saharan oases, it is a large town lying at the edge of the western foothills of the Ahaggar mountains in the heart of the Sahara. It is a busy town, the bustle resulting from its position on the trans-Saharan trading route, giving travellers like me a chance to rest and re-stock with fuel and food, and there is help to be had with the maintenance needs of the vehicle.

Thick palm groves and dense scrub clings to the town's edges and weaves a green thread into the town-centre along ditches and storm drains. Tamarisks line the streets and rows of eucalyptus shade pavements and squares. In them are olivaceous, subalpine warblers, and chiffchaffs calling, while a white-crowned black wheatear hunts insects on the ground from the vantage of the campsite wall. Sweeping above the town are handfuls of African rock or pale crag martins, but with them are lots of swallows. Some of these swallows could have wintered here, but most I suspect will be passage birds pausing on their journey north.

At the edge of town is a patch of open dusty ground littered with scrap metal and household junk. Two small boys stand idly watching a few goats rummage in the litter and there are some camels hobbled in the shade. Even here, with the noise of traffic and people passing along the pavements, there are wheatears, two or three of them working the ground from the top of rubbish piles and old tyres. Having fed here for a few days, they will continue their northward passage.

The Tedemeit Plateau is a hamada desert between the oasis towns of In Salah and El Golea in Algeria, and it ends at the southern edge of the Grand Erg Occidental. For most of the day as I have been travelling across

The pale rufous crown and nape, and lack of dark markings on the undersides suggests this is a bird of the race erlangeri, *the palest and smallest of the five races of lanner falcon. They range across north Africa to the Middle East and into the Arabian peninsula. The lanner is also distributed throughout much of Africa mostly in the semi-desert and drier savanna woodlands, but also mountainous regions and true desert in the Sahara.*

the vast gravel plain, there has been the shine of enormous sand dunes in the distance, reflected in pools of shimmering heat along the horizon – the classic image of a desert mirage. In the sudden cool of early evening as the mirage vanishes I turn off the road and head for the shelter of a narrow valley away from the road to find a place to make camp for the night.

During an early supper of boiled rice, onions and tinned fish, with plenty of tea to quench my thirst, a loose cluster of sand martins hurry by and in a while a lone white wagtail passes. Then suddenly the valley begins to echo to the distinctive rapid *kek..kek...kek..kek..kek* of a calling falcon. High up around the edge of the cliff a lanner falcon sweeps into view. In the evening stillness I can hear the rush and turbulence of air in the feathers as the falcon banks round in a tight circle and lands high above on a rock ledge.

Like the timing of breeding in Eleonora's falcon, but this time in spring, the lanner takes advantage of a transient and predictable food supply which lasts from early February to the end of April. Breeding pairs in the Tibesti Mountains have been shown to feed principally on passing yellow wagtails, hoopoes, quail and turtle doves. For the rest of the year they revert to taking mainly rodents, reptiles, beetles and grasshoppers, but they will also take birds from the small local population.

The southern edge of the desert lies 1700 kilometres behind, and the Sahara's northern edge cannot be too far away now as spiky grasses and low scrubby vegetation begins to appear in the landscape again. A change to sub-desert again is marked by the sight of a hoopoe lark. Following the road around the southern edge of the Grand Erg Occidental I reach Hassi Toueil. It is March 12th. The village, (or is it an oasis?), is a cluster of mud and rough brick buildings that fill a hollow in the rolling sands and gravel of the northern Algerian Sahara.

At the bottom of the village there is a leaky artesian well sprinkling water like a fountain through a patched and punctured hosepipe. Shaded courtyards and alleys are strung with lines of drying clothes and filled with the noise of chickens, goats and children. Behind walls and fences around the edge of the village there are planted lines of cypress and eucalyptus sheltering small patches of cultivation from the sun and wind-blown sand.

A male redstart, in bright breeding plumage, perches on a drooping palm stem and flies frequently out to catch insects in the patchy sunlight on the ground. Again the similarities in habitat that this species frequents are striking. From Lappland to the Sahel and now in the Sahara on the long journey home, each time they have been working the ground beneath a sun dappled canopy of trees. A few chiffchaffs work the smaller shrubs and I watch a tree pipit feeding along the grassy edge of an irrigation dyke.

On the southern side of Hassi Toueil is an overflow of water which spills out into the desert as an enormous fan of rivulets, patches of open water and a huge spread of damp stained mud and sand. The whole area is thick with vegetation. It looks a good site for an early morning watch.

In the half-hour before dawn there is a strong cold wind from the north-east. The moon is still bright and I work around the windward side of a

Chiffchaffs in the vegetable gardens at El Oued, an 'oasis' town in the northern Algerian Sahara. Many winter in habitats like this in the Sahara.

A rising moon over the sand dunes and palms of the northern Sahara.

high dune bank in the half-light looking for a sheltered vantage point to overlook the leaky green patch below.

Half way down the steep face of one small dune, I notice a movement around a bunch of woody shrubs, and in the dimness see an extraordinary sight. A cluster of about nine or ten swallows and a few house martins are sheltering in among the low stems, or bunched together on the surface of the sand. Having roosted together for warmth, they will be on their way again as soon as the sun appears.

As the sun rises it reveals a fine spindrift of sand streaming from the dune crests creating a gritty haze over the wet patch of desert below. In the rapidly growing light I can see a small flock of little ringed plovers feeding and a sprinkling of yellow wagtails.

I sit working for an hour or so, until the sun is well up, then I carry on down the steep slip face onto the hard gravel of the desert floor. It is then that I hear a distant and slightly feeble *pyyeeep...pyyeeep.....pyeeep ....pyeeep* call coming from somewhere out in open country to the south. Searching with binoculars I locate the calling bird as it approaches. Flying from out of the desert with powerful and steady wing beats is an osprey. It is an incredibly exciting sight. This is a bird whose progress I have roughly followed from northern Europe to West Africa, and now on the way back, but this time crossing the desert, I have met up with one again. It is exactly this kind of link that I could not plan for, but have been searching for as I have made my journey as an artist on migration. On reaching the small patches of open water the osprey turns sharply and dropping low, stoops down close to the surface in a sort of half-hearted attempt to catch something. Then circling back over the dunes it glides down to land on a narrow stony ridge jutting out into the water.

By mid-morning the osprey has gone, and walking around the edge of the damp sand I can find only one or two yellow wagtails. The little ringed plovers have gone as well, and now a small flock of trumpeter finches, local birds, are drinking at the water's edge where the plovers were. It seems that most of the migrants that were here early on have continued their journey.

The breezes turn stronger and much warmer later in the day, sending eddies of sand whirling and twisting across the desert. As I walk back towards the village, from high in the thermals above I hear a loose flapping sound like wind spilling from an untrimmed sail. Looking up, I watch five white storks spiralling rapidly down towards this wet patch of desert. With legs lowered, necks drooped and wings spilling air they drop as a tight group into a corner of shallow water. Soon they begin preening and moving slowly about the pools, but do not appear to feed.

Many of the returning Iberian and west European white storks, which have wintered in west Africa, reach the Straits of Gibraltar in late February or early March, so these few birds are on schedule. From here it is 1000 kilometres northwest – as the stork flies – to the Straits of Gibraltar.

The half a million square kilometres of North Africa from Tunisia westwards to Morocco, which is dominated by the Atlas mountains, is isolated from the rest of the African continent. It turns its back on sub-Saharan Africa and the extremes of the desert and faces Europe to share with the Mediterranean the same geological architecture, and the same temperate and changeable climate. Arab geographers called it the Djezira El Maghreb meaning 'The Island of the West'.

The climb into the Atlas mountains is slowed not only by stops to watch Moussier's redstarts and Alpine swifts, but also because the road is narrow and winding. Climbing all the time past olive groves and cultivated fields it swings tightly around boulder ravines, squeezes over bridges, twists past houses and fast flowing streams. Higher still the road winds past white painted farms and outhouses busy with tractors and donkey carts, dogs and

Cap Bon is a short thick finger of land that reaches out into the Mediterranean from the Maghreb, towards Sicily 160 km away. A ridge of hills runs down its centre and from it spreads a mosaic of fields, farms and heathland with pine woods and boggy hollows; beyond that is a coastal strip of sand dunes covered in places by pine woods and a thick scrub of mostly junipers and bright yellow stands of broom in flower.

chickens. Figures cloaked and hooded against the cold stand along the roadside watching flocks of sheep graze the rough ground of the verges.

Further up, past pine woods on hillsides and air scented with thyme, it turns even colder. By the time I reach the level plateaus on the top, I have put on all the warm clothing I have got.

Unlike the gradual changes in landscapes and birds that I have noted over the past months in Africa, here in the low Atlas mountains of the Maghreb the change is sudden and profound. What has previously been slowly detectable by latitude is now suddenly apparent by altitude. In less than a day I have moved from the marchlands of the Sahara to familiar green meadows, orchards and fields of winter sown cereals. The birds also indicate the significance of the change. Serins, with a shrill tingling call like a cheap charm bracelet being rattled, display from surrounding trees; a robin calls from the cover of a prickly pear, and there are chaffinches in an orchard of almond trees. There are skylarks and corn buntings on the telegraph wires and fence posts, and goldfinches on the verges. Although I am still on the African landmass, the Sahel and Sahara and their migrants, although only a few days behind me, seem much more than a continent away. Sometime in the past few hours I seem to have crossed from the Tropics to the Temperate zone. The landscape and the birds now have a distinctive 'Europeanness'. Welcome 'home'!

CHAPTER TWELVE

Journey's End

Around the coast of North Norfolk are large areas of man-made landscape reclaimed from the sea. Long, straight, sharp-edged ditches divide huge angular fields. Here and there are isolated corners filled by low scrub and rough ground, with a willow or two, or a line of poplars to break the flatness of the landscape.

It is now late morning on a day at the very end of April. The wind is cold from the east, but the sun has climbed enough to occasionally break through the grey mist and low cloud that has lingered all morning. For some time I have been sitting at the edge of a raised track overlooking some coastal fields watching a very special bird. A Montagu's harrier.

For the past half-hour, the male has been flying low over the ground, backwards and forwards over a prospective nest site, sometimes dropping down to be lost in the grass for a while, then suddenly appearing again and flying off on short excursions over the surrounding fields and ditches. A female marsh harrier passes, and when it moves close to the Montagu's he comes out of the grass but does not mob the marsh harrier. Instead he flies parallel to it for a short distance before turning back to his 'patch' in the grass.

In Britain Montagu's harrier is a very rare breeding bird. Last year 18 young were reared from just 8 nests and all of the sites are wardened to protect them from disturbance and the scourge of egg thieves.

In a while the male Montagu's rises up again, but this time makes a few tight circles over the nest site and climbing fast drifts inland, until, as a faint speck, it is lost to view. It is a long time before anything else happens, but then suddenly a female Montagu's appears in the neighbourhood. She begins to drift around the area where the male had been earlier, then she disappears into the grass. But still no sign of the male. When he does appear the change in his behaviour is extreme, and quite magical. From high up he plummets in a steep power-dive at the female that by now is up in the air again. He twists and turns, diving around her, then rises up, circles once or twice and dives again. The intensity of this 'sky-dancing' behaviour and the time of year suggest that the female has only very recently arrived at the site. The male will have arrived back from Africa a week or so earlier, normally they are not back much before mid-April, and would have started prospecting a nest site almost immediately; now he is drawing the female's attention to it.

This nuptial 'sky-dancing' display is beautiful enough, but there is added

The Montagu's sky-dancing display.

excitement for me in watching these harriers. I remember late last summer sitting in almost the same spot painting what are possibly the same pair. I watched them hunting and returning to the nest with food for the youngster already on the wing. I saw many Montagu's in Africa and I got to know it well as a species. Now, after their long journey, and mine too, I feel I can unashamedly share in their display of 'excitement' at being 'home'. Descriptions of it as a long-distance migrant that winters in Africa south of the Sahara, now has a very special meaning for me.

It is now early May and two weeks have passed since I was with the Montagu's harriers in eastern Britain. Now I am at Stapelholm, a large area of flood-meadows, carr and fen vegetation that spreads between the Eider and Treene rivers where they flow through the western side of Schleswig Holstein in what was the Federal Republic of Germany. It is a landscape of willow, alder and silver birch, sedgy hollows, and reed filled ditches subdivided by rough meadows filled with cattle. The landscape around Stapelholm has a 'timeless' and untouched look about it, There are black-tailed godwits displaying, willow warblers singing and cuckoos calling.

There are other bird sounds characteristic of damp grassland – the sliding whistle of curlew, the fluted piping of lapwings, drumming snipe, and deep down in a sedgy hollow a grasshopper warbler starting up its unmistakable,

White storks at Bergenhusen. Between 1974 and 1984 the number of breeding storks in Germany declined by 71%. Habitat loss and agricultural changes are partly to blame, as are the problems white storks face in Africa.

seamless reeling and ratchet-like call. In the distance are two white storks soundlessly stalking through a meadow. These are the birds I have come to see at the village of Bergenhusen on the edge of the low scarp above the damp meadows. The village has a sign on its outskirts proclaiming, 'Willkommen im Storchenparadies'; it is said that Bergenhusen is the 'Stork capital' of Europe.

In many parts of Europe storks nest close to human habitation and traditionally are encouraged to do so. In Bergenhusen platforms are placed on roofs, strapped around chimneys or fixed to the tops of lamp-posts to ensure that the storks have plenty of possible nesting sites. Some platforms are

The view in the evening across the polders towards Zaanstad in Holland.

fixed like saddles over the apex of tiled roofs. There are broken platforms and dilapidated nests unused in years and green with moss. Perhaps the long association that the white stork has had with man, and its arrival back from Africa heralding the coming of summer and better times, is a reason for the notion that storks bring babies and new life. With one artificial nest site on the top of the restaurant in the village centre looking like a wicker cradle, it is possible to believe that the story might be true!

Despite centuries of reclamation, drainage and enclosure, there are still parts of the low-lying Dutch landscape that remain permanently waterlogged. Trembling polders, damp meadows and marshes are divided up by webs of dykes and ditches, with small windmills on almost every polder corner. In summer these sodden patches are home to many characteristic wetland birds, many of them migrants; black-tailed godwits, yellow wagtails, garganey, and a host of warblers arriving to breed. But the classic bird of these damp landscapes, and the one that interests me most, is the ruff, particularly the contrast between the flocks of thousands that I saw in West Africa during the winter and their patchy distribution and rarity over most of western Europe in the summer. Once, there were thought to be about 10,000 breeding pairs of Ruff in the Netherlands, which by the early 1950s had dropped to about 6000 pairs. Now there are perhaps only 1000 pairs remaining. The early decline was caused as much by the demands of the gourmet trade as by the draining of marshland and

Examples of the variation in ruff breeding plumage. Birds with predominantly white ear-tufts and ruffs are 'satellite' males, and darker birds are 'independent' males. The difference denotes their social status and behaviour at the lek. 'Independents' occupy and defend territory, or court. 'Satellites' hold no territory but are tolerated at court and their behaviour is much more opportunistic.

wetland habitats, but in the 20th century it is certainly habitat loss which has led to its continued decline and often extinction over many parts of its former European range. It is also the contrast between winter and summer plumage and behaviour of the ruff that intrigues me.

In late March the males are the first to arrive back and within two weeks most have assembled at the special display arena or lekking site. Towards the middle of April the females, or reeves, begin arriving and are attracted to the lek for mating, drawn by the spectacular ornamentation of the male's plumage and by the bizarre antics of their stereotyped posturing and display 'dances' performed like some mediaeval jousting tournament.

Ilperveld, a fragment of ancient undrained wetland not far from Amsterdam, is a reserve of the Nederlandse Vereniging tot Bescherming van Vogels. The warden Nico Dekker has marked the best lekking site on a map and has also lent me a boat to wander these ancient waterways.

With a clear horizon and only thin wisps of high cloud lit by the first

Ruff at the lek, a word derived from the Swedish word leka, *meaning to play.*

glimmers of daylight, I head out slowly through the watery maze of channels. Curious bullocks follow as I steer the boat cautiously down the narrow corridors of rich dark peaty brown water. Black-tailed godwits rise from the polders as I pass and, hanging in the wind above the boat, call noisily as they follow my passage through their territory. There are redshank and lapwings, meadow pipits and yellow wagtails, herons, shovellers and tufted duck, common terns and a marsh harrier as well. Swallows pause for a while on the rusty cables of an abandoned dredger run into the dyke bank, and there is a wheatear using the iron work as a vantage and I float past a cuckoo fluttering a little clumsily in the top of some reeds.

The lekking area is visible some way off. A long lip of one polder bank has patches of bare earth, trampled grass stools and worn clumps of sedge and taller meadow grasses. A lone ruff is feeding as I approach, so cutting the engine and drifting with the wind I run up against the opposite bank. Tying up to a paddle pushed deep into the soft mud, I unpack my sketching tools and settle in the boat to wait. Within minutes and without a sound four more ruff arrive in quick succession on the lek and almost immediately the display begins. What follows is an extraordinary tournament, or sequence of ritualised posturings, struttings, stabbings, dances and mock battles which continue for almost an hour. The strangest part of the lek display is that it is performed in total silence, the only sound coming from the flap of feather ruffs and wings, like the sound of washing fluttering on a line in the breeze.

A sand martin colony in Cambridgeshire. Sand martins show a considerable degree of fidelity, both to an area and a colony.

After mating the reeves make nests in the surrounding fields and meadows where they incubate the eggs and raise the young in almost total isolation from the ruff.

The way back to the mooring by the warden's house is marked by the mobbing godwits and the bullocks on the bank, but this time there is a singing whinchat, even larger numbers of swifts and swallows sweeping above the polders, then a hobby suddenly appears; the familiar superb scythe-shaped silhouette dashing across the warm and cloudless late afternoon sky.

Before I began my journey I had a rough idea of the contrasts that might be part of a ruff's annual breeding, wintering and migration cycle. But checking through my notes and sketches, now that I am almost home, I know for certain that the real picture is far more dramatic and exciting. The same is true of the many other migrants I have got to know well, like Montagu's harrier, osprey, yellow wagtail and wheatear. As an artist with a love of landscape and a naturalist's interest in birds I have attempted to sketch a broad outline their stories. Without contributing anything new to the science of ornithology, I have simply added colour and a little detail to the familiar field-guide information such as; hobby (*Falco subbuteo*). Migrant; breeding in Boreal to Warm Temperate zones, wintering in Subtropical zone, mainly in African savannas south of the Sahara.

Now, late at night, I am working out in the studio which stands at the bottom of the garden, overlooking open fields and a small hawthorn thicket. For the past half-hour a cuckoo has been calling in the darkness from somewhere among the hawthorns. When it is time to go indoors, I tidy my paints and brushes, turn out the light, and stepping outside lock the door. The sky is clear and there is a three-quarter moon; pausing on the path for a while I listen. In the absolute stillness of the early summer night the call carries far and wide, and will sure to be heard by any female passing overhead in the near darkness. Tomorrow morning, if he is still active in the thicket, I will go across there and try and get some sketches. If not, I will visit my patch near the village to check up on 'my' hobbies. One is 'home' already and I will go up there when I can until they and their young depart once more for Africa.

General Reading List

Alerstam, T. *Bird Migration*. Cambridge University Press 1990.
Armstrong, E.O. *The Folklore of Birds*. Collins 1958
Baker, R. *Bird Navigation: the solution of a mystery?* Hodder and Stoughton 1984
Baker, R. *The Mystery of Migration*. Macdonald 1980
Brown, L., Urban, E. K., Newman. K. *et al. The Birds of Africa Vols. I II & III*. Academic Press 1986 –
Cade, T. & Digby, R.D. *Falcons of the World* Collins 1982
Campbell, B. & Lack, E. (eds). *A Dictionary of Birds*. Calton (Poyser) and Vermillin (Buteo) 1985
Carr, N. *Valley of the Elephants*. Collins 1979
Chernov, Y. I. *The Living Tundra*. Cambridge University Press 1985
Christian, G.O. *Down the Long Wind* Newnes 1961
Cloudsley-Thompson, J. L. *Terrestrial Environments* Croom Helm 1975
Cramp, S., *et al. The Birds of the Western Palearctic* Vols. I II III IV & V. Oxford University Press 1977 -
Curry-Lindhal, K. *Europe, a Natural History* Hamish Hamilton 1964
Dorst, J. *The Migration of Birds* Heinemann 1962
Durman, R. *Bird Observatories in Britain and Ireland* T & A.D. Poyser 1976
Eckholm, E., Foley, G., Barnard, G. & Timberlake, L. *Fuelwood: the energy crisis that won't go away* Earthscan 1984
Elkins, N. *Weather and Bird Behaviour* T. & A.D. Poyser 1983
Grey of Fallodon, Edward Grey, Viscount. *The Charm of Birds* Hodder and Stoughton 1937
Fisher, J. *The Shell Bird Book* Ebury Press and Michael Joseph 1966
Grainger, A. *Desertification* Earthscan 1982
Harrison, C.J.O. *An Atlas of the Birds of the Western Palearctic* Collins 1982
Harrison-Church, R. J. *West Africa – a study of the environment and man's use of it* Longman 1974
Hayman, P., Marchant, J. & Prater, T. *Shorebirds – an identification guide to the waders of the world* Croom Helm 1986
Hibbert, C. *Africa Explored, Europeans in the dark continent 1769-1889* Allen Lane 1982
Houston, J. M. *The Western Mediterranean World* Longman 1964
Hutchinson, C.D *Ireland's Wetlands and their Birds* Irish Wildbird Conservancy 1979
Ingersoll, E. *Birds in Legend, Fable and Folklore* Longmans 1923
Jensen, J. V. & Kirkeby, J. *The Birds of The Gambia* Aros (Nature Guides) 1980
Lack, P. *The Atlas of Wintering Birds in Britain and Ireland* T. & A.D. Poyser 1986
Mackworth-Praed, C. W. & Grant, C. H. B. *African Handbook of Birds Series I II & III* Longman 1970 & 1973
Madge, S. and Burn, H. *Wildfowl – an identification guide to the ducks, geese and swans of the world* Christopher Helm 1988
Mead, C. *Bird Migration* Country Life 1983
Moreau, R. E. D. *The Bird Faunas of Africa and its Islands* Academic Press 1966
Moreau, R. E. D. *The Palearctic – African Bird Migration Systems* Academic Press 1972
Morgan, W. T. W. *East Africa* Longman 1973
Ogilvie, M. A. D. *Wild Geese* T. & A. D. Poyser 1978
Porter, R. F. D., Willis, I., Christensen, S. & Nielsen, B. P. *Flight Identification of European Raptors* T. & A. D. Poyser 1981
Prater, A. J. *Estuary Birds of Britain and Ireland* T. & A. D. Poyser 1981
Sage, B. *The Arctic and its Wildlife* Croom Helm 1986
Sharrock, J. T. R. *The Atlas of Breeding Birds in Britain and Ireland* T. & A. D. Poyser 1976
Simms, E. *British Warblers* Collins 1985
Swift, J. *The Sahara* Time-Life Books
Timberlake, L. *Afica in Crisis* Earthscan 1985
Walter, H. *Eleonora's Falcon. Adaptions to Prey and Habitat in a Social Raptor* University of Chicago Press 1979
Wyllie, I. *The Cuckoo* Shire Natural History 1987
Young Ornithologists Club. *Spring Migration Phone-In Reports 1983-1988*

Index

Rather than being comprehensive, this index lists only significant mentions of bird species (many species mentioned in the text are not included here), along with selected topics, names of people, countries and certain well-known localities.